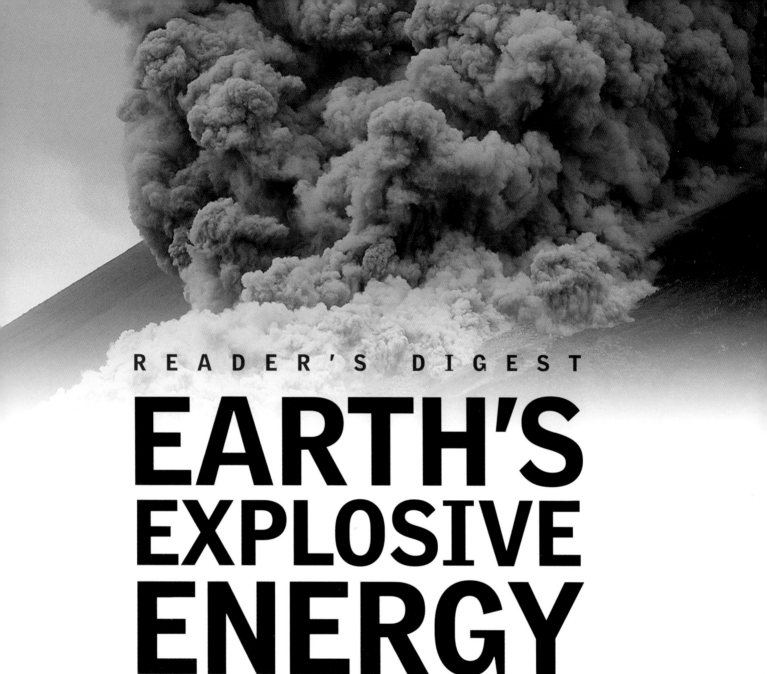

READER'S DIGEST

EARTH'S EXPLOSIVE ENERGY

1999 AVALANCHE

1999 AUSTRIA

A gigantic powder snow avalanche sweeps into the Alpine skiing resort of Galtür, travelling at some 200 km/h. It overturns cars, destroys seven modern buildings and buries more than 55 people, of whom fewer than half survive.

2000 EARTHQUAKE

2000 INDONESIA

A series of earthquakes rocks the region of Bengkulu City in southern Sumatra – the largest has a Richter magnitude of 7.9. The quakes cause extensive damage and landslides, destroying 1800 houses an killing 103 people.

Island

stic
s and

s 600 or so
about a quarter
ant eruptions during
5. On average, about
rld's volcanoes
ss of erupting
e time.

FASCINATING FACT

Between 1996 and 2005, there were more than 150 earthquakes with a Richter magnitude of 7.0 or greater. These are major earthquakes, affecting areas more than 160 km across and capable of causing serious damage when they strike populated centres.

• 1996 ICELAND •

• 2005 CHINA

1999 AUSTRIA •

2002 ITALY •

• 2004 INDIAN OCEAN

2001 EL SALVADOR • • 1997 MONTSERRAT
• 1998 NICARAGUA

• 2000 INDONESIA

• 2003 SOLOMON ISLANDS

1998 NICARAGUA

Intense rainfall during Hurricane Mitch saturates the Casita volcano. One of its flanks disintegrates into a lahar – a torrent of ash and water. Within 3 minutes, this kills 2000 people as it smashes through two towns.

1998 LAHAR

PYROCLASTIC FLOW

1997

1997 MONTSERRAT

The Soufrière Hills volcano on the Caribbean of Montserrat erupts with great violence, producing a devastating series of pyrocla flows – fast-moving mixtures of hot ga ash. These kill 23 people and severel damage hundreds of homes.

Of the world active volcanoes, exploded with signific the decade 1996-200 20-25 of the wo are in the proce at any o

FASCINATING FACT

1996 OUTBURST FLOOD

1996 ICELAND

A volcanic caldera erupts beneath a large ice-cap, called Vatnajökull, in south-eastern Iceland. The ice-cap melts partially and releases a terrifying onslaught of floodwater known as a *jökulhlaup* (outburst flood).

THE EARTH'S INTERIOR COLOSSAL AMOUNTS CAN EXPLODE WITH THE PLANET'S INTERNAL OF NUCLEAR FORCES – STRAIN ENERGY IN THE EARTHQUAKES. GRAVITY AND AVALANCHES. WILL CONTROL THE DANGERS

AND SURFACE STORE
OF ENERGY THAT
SPECTACULAR POWER.
HEAT – THE PRODUCT
FUELS VOLCANOES.
CRUST IS BEHIND
DRIVES LANDSLIDES
WE EVER BE ABLE TO
OF THESE FORCES?

2005 METHANE

2004 TSUNAMI

2005 CHINA

A methane gas explosion in China results in one of the most deadly mining accidents in recent history. It happens some 240 m underground in a coal mine at Fuxin City, Liaoning Province, and leaves 214 people dead.

...ples
...all places
...o means
...d climate
...adlines.

2004 INDIAN OCEAN

A devastating tsunami sweeps across the Indian Ocean, generated by a gigantic earthquake, with a Richter magnitude of 9.2, along a section of seafloor between Sumatra and the Andaman Islands. The tsunami causes more than 225 000 fatalities, concentrated in Indonesia, Sri Lanka, India and Thailand.

On top of the 225 000 deaths from the Indian Ocean tsunami, more than 200 000 people died between 1996 and 2005 as a result of earthquakes, avalanches, mudslides and other types of landslide, volcanic eruptions and gas explosions in mines.

FASCINATING FACT

LAVA FLOW

2003 SUBMARINE ERUPTION

2003 SOLOMON ISLANDS

The underwater volcano Kavachi erupts, leading to the sudden and dramatic appearance of a new island, 15 m high, at the seas' surface. Within three months, the island has subsided once more beneath the waves.

EXPLOSIVE DECADE

EVERY YEAR, EARTH'S RESTLESS ENERGY IS RELEASED IN DESTRUCTIVE AND OFTEN DEADLY EVENTS AROUND THE GLOBE. These are a few exam of different types of explosive event in the decade from 1996 to 2005. Not around the world are at equal risk of experiencing such disasters – and by all outbursts of Earth's energy result in disaster. But as populations rise an change continues, such dramatic events are increasingly likely to hit the he

2001 LANDSLIDE

2002 ITALY

Europe's highest volcano, Etna, on the island of Sicily, becomes noticeably more active, producing an enormous cloud of ash and spectacular lava flows. One of these incinerates a tourist station.

2002

2001 EL SALVADOR

An earthquake triggers a landslide, in which some 30 000 m³ of loose, predominantly dry soil slides down a steep escarpment at the edge of Santa Tecla, a suburb of San Salvador. The wall of earth rampages through a residential area, causing more than 580 fatalities.

EARTH'S EXPLOSIVE ENERGY

1 MOVING PLATES

16 THE HEAT ENGINE
20 TECTONIC PLATES
22 PLATE BOUNDARIES
30 RING OF FIRE
32 MEASURING PLATE MOVEMENTS
34 PLATES AND EVOLUTION

2 SHAKING EARTH

38 CAUSES OF QUAKES
42 DETECTION AND MEASUREMENT
44 COURSE OF A QUAKE
50 DEADLY QUAKES
54 SUBMARINE QUAKES
56 PREDICTION AND CONTROL
58 BUILDING PROTECTION

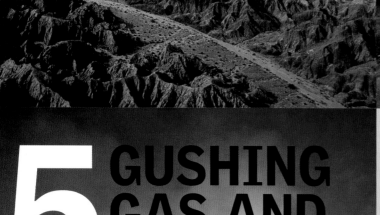

5 GUSHING GAS AND WATER

110 HOT SPRINGS AND GEYSERS
116 MUD VOLCANOES
118 EXPLODING LAKES
120 METHANE MENACE
122 GLACIER OUTBURST FLOODS
126 TIDAL BORES

6 MOVING EARTH, ICE AND SNOW

130 LANDSLIDES
136 RIVERS OF MUD
140 WHITE DANGER
144 PLUMMETING ICE

3 WHEN EARTH ERUPTS

62 WHAT IS A VOLCANO?
66 TYPES OF VOLCANO
70 ERUPTION STYLES
74 LAVA FLOWS
78 AIRBORNE HAZARDS
80 PYROCLASTIC FLOWS AND SURGES
82 RIFT VOLCANOES
84 SUPER-VOLCANOES
86 KILLER ERUPTIONS
90 LIVING WITH VOLCANOES

4 ISLANDS NEW

96 SITTING ON A HOTSPOT
100 VOLCANIC ISLAND ARCS
104 AN ISLAND IS BORN

7 FORCES AND ENERGY

148 FUNDAMENTAL FORCES
150 EARTH'S ENERGY AND GRAVITY
152 NUCLEAR FORCES
154 ELECTROMAGNETIC FORCE

INTRODUCTION

TRAPPED IN THE INTERIOR OF THE EARTH ARE COLOSSAL STORES OF PENT-UP ENERGY. Some of this energy is contained within the planet's core and mantle and in the fiery magma that wells up in 'hotspots' beneath its rocky crust. Some is held in combustible substances, including fossil fuels, that saturate the layers of the crust. And some is in the form of mechanical strain energy that builds up around the edges of the interlocking tectonic plates of the planet's outer shell. Features on the Earth's surface, such as mountain lakes and glaciers, snow-covered summits and the contoured hills, cliffs and mountains themselves, hold mind-boggling amounts of energy in a form called gravitational potential energy.

All these types of **stored energy** are released from time to time at the Earth's surface, sometimes in tumultuous and lethal fashion. Recent examples include the **volcanic eruption** that rocked **Mount St Helens** in the USA in 1990; the **earthquake** and subsequent fires that devastated the Japanese city of **Kobe** in 1995; the powder snow **avalanche** – a wall of 'white death' – that descended on the Austrian ski resort of **Galtür** in 1999; and, most disastrous of all, the Indian Ocean earthquake and **tsunami** of 2004. Other dangerous

releases of the Earth's energy include rock falls, **landslides**, lahars (highly fluid mudflows), glacier outburst floods or *jökulhlaups*, explosions of natural gas in coalmines, and the sudden discharge of vast quantities of carbon dioxide gas from particular African lakes. Equally spectacular but less dangerous to human life are **geysers** and hot springs; the curious oozings of gas, earth, oil and salty water known as mud volcanoes; and **submarine volcanoes** that explode out of the sea to form new islands.

The production, storage and unleashing of these expressions of the Earth's energy can be traced back to **four fundamental forces** that underpin all activity in the natural world. These forces are **gravity**, which plays a vital role in phenomena from tectonic plate movements to avalanches; the **electromagnetic force**, which controls the storage and release of chemical energy; and the strong and weak **nuclear forces** that are key to the continuous production of heat within the Earth through radioactive decay. As a result of these enduring forces, sudden explosive releases of energy will continue to occur at the Earth's surface as often and with as much intensity as in the past. The challenge is to find new ways of **predicting** such outbursts and of **harnessing** the restless **energy** behind them.

MOVING PLATES

1

THE EARTH'S ROCKY OUTER SHELL, THE LITHOSPHERE, IS COMPOSED OF IMMENSE SOLID STRUCTURES CALLED TECTONIC PLATES. These never stay still. Slowly, but continuously, they shift around, driven by heat flows emanating from the planet's interior. Many of the natural energy releases that take place at the Earth's surface – especially earthquakes and volcanic eruptions – occur around the boundaries between these plates, as they grind past, dip beneath or collide with the edges of neighbouring plates. Most of the boundaries are submarine, as here (left) in the North Atlantic near Iceland. Others are visible as gigantic faults running across the land surface. In many locations, the interactions at these boundaries have produced dramatic features, such as uplifted mountain ranges and lines of volcanoes.

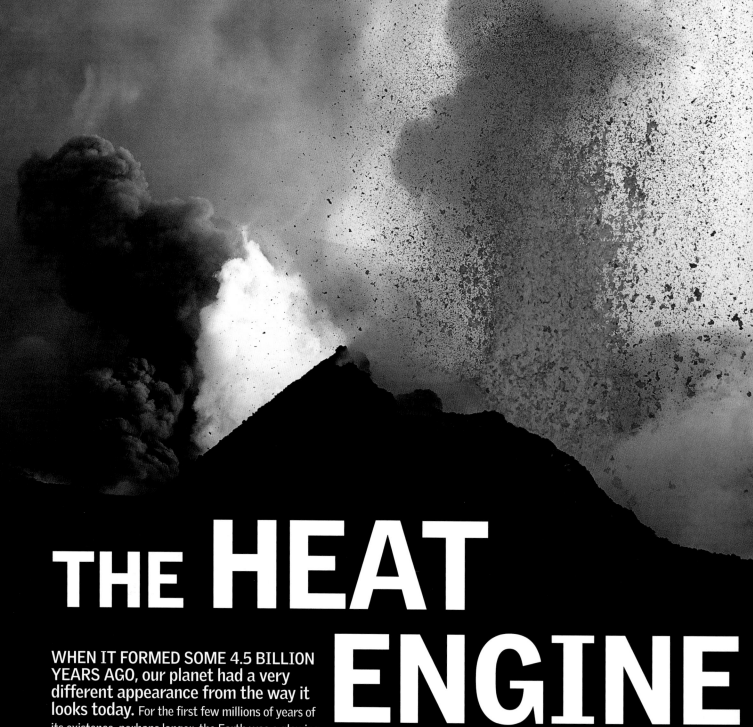

THE HEAT ENGINE

WHEN IT FORMED SOME 4.5 BILLION YEARS AGO, our planet had a very different appearance from the way it looks today. For the first few millions of years of its existence, perhaps longer, the Earth was a glowing, seething ball of mostly liquid material, with an average temperature measured in thousands of degrees centigrade. At its surface, this literal 'hell on Earth' was in a state of constant flux, racked by frequent explosions, eruptions of noxious gases and jets of fiery liquid.

The source of Earth's heat

What caused the early Earth to be so hot and fiery? What was the source of the colossal amount of heat energy that it possessed? The answers to these questions lie primarily in the way that Earth and all the other planets in the Solar System were formed – through the gradual accretion of countless billions of small dust particles (together with considerable quantities of gas) that existed in a disc-shaped cloud around the precursor of today's Sun. These particles were drawn together by gravity. In doing so they converted gravitational or potential energy – the energy that an object possesses by virtue of its separation from other objects – into energy of

MAGMA FOUNTAIN A volcano is a vent on Earth's surface through which magma (molten rock) and hot gases can escape. It is a direct route that Earth's internal heat can take to reach the surface – at times, explosively.

movement, called kinetic energy. As each dust particle collided with others to create larger particles, kinetic energy was released as heat. These larger particles would then also collide, producing ever-bigger objects. Heat energy gradually accumulated as many billions of collisions continued to occur – and the size of the particles and the violence of collisions increased – creating what might be termed a 'heat ball' effect.

In the early stages of its formation, Earth was much less compact than it is today. The accretionary process led to a steadily increasing gravitational pull throughout the planet, gradually contracting it into a smaller volume. This process of compaction converted more gravitational energy into heat energy, raising Earth's temperature further. Heat conducts slowly through rock, so the build-up of this internal heat source was not balanced by an equal loss of heat from the Earth's surface.

Even after the planet had reached approximately the size it is today, for a long period – up to an estimated 600 million years – large asteroids and comets flying around the Solar System continued to bombard it regularly. Each impact from one of these bodies generated more heat. In addition, around 40 million years after its first formation, Earth is thought to have been struck by a Mars-sized object – an episode that eventually gave rise to the Moon. This collision

would also have generated a tremendous amount of heat, and for a considerable period following the impact Earth was probably almost completely molten.

Additional heat generators

Two other processes contributed to Earth's primordial heat. The first of these derived from Earth's 'compositional sorting'. During the phases of Earth's early history when it was partially or completely liquid, the chemical elements that make up the planet were redistributed by gravity. Heavier elements such as iron and nickel sank towards the centre of the planet; lighter elements such as silicon and oxygen floated up towards the surface and eventually became important components of Earth's rocky crust. These movements caused an overall redistribution of mass, which again generated heat through the conversion of gravitational energy into heat energy.

A second additional heat generator – one that still operates today, though at diminished intensity – was radioactive

MOLTEN SURFACE A lava lake on Erta Ale in Ethiopia is covered by a skin of solidified lava. Disturbances in the magma tear this skin into huge panels separated by incandescent fissures.

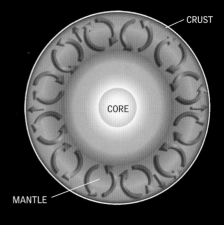

EARTH'S INTERNAL HEAT FLOW
Earth has three layers – a very hot metallic core, a mantle consisting of semi-molten rocky material and a cooler outer rocky layer called the crust. Heat drains outwards from the core partly by conduction (particle to particle) and partly by convective heat flows that operate through slow, circular movements of the semi-molten material in the mantle.

CRUST

CORE

MANTLE

decay. Scattered throughout the Earth's interior from the time of its original formation are a number of unstable radioactive isotopes, notably some long-lived isotopes of the elements uranium, thorium and potassium. As each atom of one of these isotopes decays, it gives off a tiny amount of heat (see pages 152-153). The number of these atoms is so vast that the total amount of heat generated is considerable. The rate of internal heat generation by radioactive decay during Earth's early years is estimated at approximately 40 terawatts (40 trillion watts). Today, because a proportion of the initial radioactive load has already converted to stable, non-radioactive substances, the rate of energy generation has dropped to about 24 terawatts. This is still a huge amount of power – about 50 per cent more than the total rate of human global energy consumption.

Effects of the heat engine

Since its fiery beginning, Earth has been cooling from the outside inwards. This has been a slow process, because the loss of heat energy into space has largely been offset by continuing internal heat generation through radioactive decay. For much of the past 4 billion years, the planet's outer layer, its crust, has been relatively cool, but the central regions of the planet are still extremely hot, with an estimated central core temperature of 5000–7000°C.

The immense amount of heat energy still present in the Earth's core continues to escape. This is now known to occur mainly through an extremely large-scale, slow, convective process driven by the Earth's core heat. Rock in the lower parts of Earth's mantle (the intermediate layer between the core and crust) is warmed by heat from the core, causing it to soften, expand and rise towards the surface. In other parts of the mantle cooled rock sinks, producing an overall circular movement of rising and sinking material in the mantle. A significant effect of this process is that it contributes to the movement of the

For much of the past 4 billion years, the planet's outer layer, its crust, has been relatively cool, but the centre is still extremely hot, with an estimated core temperature of 5000–7000°C.

sections or plates that make up the Earth's solid outer layer (see pages 20-21). A considerable part of the energy dissipation occurs in slowly pushing these plates around the Earth's surface. In doing so, tremendous amounts of energy are released in a variety of dynamic and explosive events at the boundaries between plates – notably in earthquakes and volcanoes.

A second effect of the convective process is that in some areas of the mantle massive plumes of extremely hot, melted rock called magma are brought towards the Earth's surface. This magma collects in vast chambers a few kilometres beneath the surface, forming what are termed 'hotspots'. These hotspots are the cause of a variety of features, including supervolcanoes such as Lake Toba in Sumatra; hotspot islands such as the Hawaiian Islands; and geothermal hot springs, which are found in many volcanic regions, such as Iceland and Japan. Supervolcanoes, of which only a handful exist in the world, are theoretically capable of quite cataclysmic eruptions – big enough to cover continent-sized areas of the planet in volcanic ash and lava and to bring about radical climate change.

Geothermal power

Although the dissipation of Earth's heat energy through disruptive forces such as earthquakes and volcanic eruptions might seem a negative factor for inhabitants of the Earth, the heat engine is also a potential positive asset as a source of reliable, non-polluting 'green' energy. If the heat from Earth's interior was spread over the whole surface of the planet, it would average about 75 watts – enough to power a lightbulb – per 1000 m². In practice, the heat flow is not spread evenly over the surface but is concentrated in particular areas – around the boundaries of tectonic plates, in volcanoes and hotspots.

The energy that can be obtained by tapping the heat flowing from Earth's interior and converting it into electricity is called geothermal energy. Currently, over 20 countries around the world – including the USA, New Zealand, Italy, Iceland, Mexico, the Philippines, Indonesia and Japan – extract this energy. In total it provides approximately 10 gigawatts of power – about 0.07 per cent of the world's energy needs.

Most geothermal energy today is extracted from areas where magma comes within a few kilometres of Earth's surface. In the near future, technological advances should allow heat energy to be extracted on an economic basis in many more areas by drilling deeper boreholes – up to 10 km or more. If the energy required to sink the boreholes is excluded, the process of generating geothermal electricity releases negligible amounts of greenhouse gases. This suggests that geothermal power may become progressively more significant in meeting human global energy needs.

THE TEMPERATURE 100 KM BELOW EARTH'S SURFACE is around 1000°–1200°C. At this temperature, many minerals in rock are close to their melting points and the rock is soft enough to flow. Vesuvius's lava melts at around 1050°C under ordinary pressure.

99 PER CENT of Earth's mass is hotter than 1000°C; less than 1 per cent is cooler than 100°C.

74 PER CENT OF EARTH'S HEAT LOSS occurs through plate activity and 9 per cent through hotspots; the remaining 17 per cent is heat lost from radioactive decay in the crust.

FACTS

THE GEYSERS

THE WORLD'S LARGEST GEOTHERMAL FIELD,

KNOWN AS THE GEYSERS, is located about 145 km north of San Francisco, in California. Consisting of a complex of 21 power plants, The Geysers is capable of continuously generating enough electricity to power around 1 million American homes.

The heat energy converted into electricity at The Geysers comes from magma lying more than 6.5 km beneath the surface. Heat is carried by radiation and conduction to layers of rock lying nearer the surface, where it heats a reservoir of water lying within cracks and pores in the rock. The resulting steam is trapped by an overlying layer of rock, called 'cap rock'. A series of wells, some more than 3 km deep, have been drilled through this rock layer to tap the steam, which is then piped to The Geysers' power plants. There, after being cleansed of tiny particles of rock, the steam is used to power turbine generators, so creating electricity – the turbines are designed to operate with steam at a temperature of 177°C and a pressure of 690 kilopascals. After passing through the turbines, the steam is cooled and turned back into water, about 25 per cent of which is pumped back into the subterranean water reservoir.

One of the advantages of The Geysers and other geothermal power plants is that they produce a steady and reliable supply of electricity. This is in contrast to some other environmentally friendly power sources, such as wind and tidal energy, whose energy output is episodic. Currently, The Geysers accounts for about a quarter of the green power produced in California.

VITAL STATISTICS

AREA: 78 km²
LOCATION: Mayacamas Mountains, near Santa Rosa, California
DISCOVERED: 1847, by William Bell Elliot
POWER GENERATION: 0.85 gigawatts (850 million watts)
FOSSIL-FUEL EQUIVALENCE: 65 million barrels of oil per year

TECTONIC PLATES

EARTH'S OUTERMOST LAYER OF ROCKY MATERIAL IS CALLED THE CRUST. There are two different types. Oceanic crust, found underneath the oceans, is 5–10 km thick and composed primarily of a dense, dark volcanic rock called basalt. Continental crust, which forms dry land, is 20–70 km thick and composed mostly of lighter rocks, such as granite. The crust, together with the uppermost part of Earth's mantle, forms a solid shell called the lithosphere.

Plates in motion

The lithosphere ranges in depth from 50 to 150 km and is broken into irregularly shaped chunks, called plates, which fit together to cover Earth's surface. These ride on top of a softer, less rigid layer of rock, the asthenosphere, which extends to a depth of about 220 km. Altogether some 100 or so plates are now recognised – seven gigantic ones, such as the Pacific Plate and Eurasian Plate, nine or ten medium-sized ones, such as the Arabian Plate, and more than 80 very small plates known as microplates. The plates all move slowly relative to each other and to the underlying mantle.

At one time, scientists believed that large-scale convection currents in the Earth's mantle drove plate motion. It was thought that the mantle currents dragged the overlying lithosphere along by friction. Although this model is still partly accepted, it is no longer thought feasible that lithospheric plates can be dragged along purely by friction, and other mechanisms are believed to contribute.

One of these, called 'ridge-push', is the process by which new lithosphere builds up at mid-ocean ridges (see pages 22-24) and pushes existing lithosphere away through the effects of gravity. Another mechanism is known as 'slab-pull'. As oceanic lithosphere moves away from the spreading ridge where it was created, it cools and becomes denser. By the time it eventually reaches a subduction zone (see page 27), it is denser than the underlying asthenosphere and sinks, dragging the plate along. This sinking of lithosphere at subduction zones is now thought to be the main driving force behind plate motion.

SAN ANDREAS FAULT

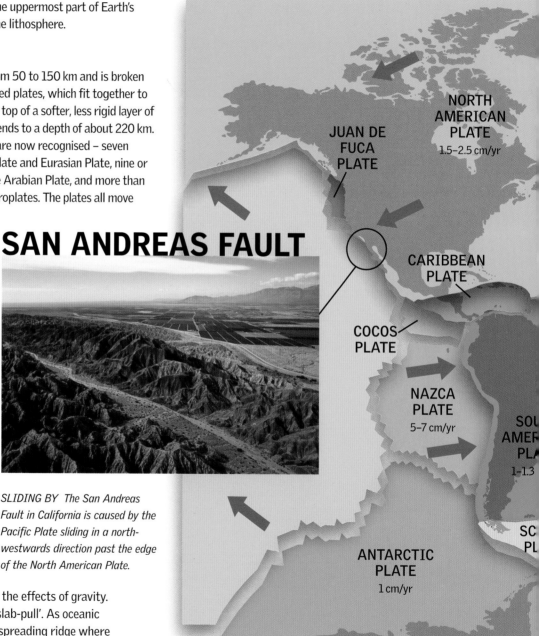

SLIDING BY The San Andreas Fault in California is caused by the Pacific Plate sliding in a north-westwards direction past the edge of the North American Plate.

NORTH AMERICAN PLATE
1.5–2.5 cm/yr

JUAN DE FUCA PLATE

CARIBBEAN PLATE

COCOS PLATE

NAZCA PLATE
5–7 cm/yr

SOU AMER PLA
1–1.3

SC PL

ANTARCTIC PLATE
1 cm/yr

GIANT JIGSAW The map shows the Earth's main tectonic plates, their directions and rates of movement and the boundaries between them. Some plates rotate slightly as they move. Plates composed largely of oceanic lithosphere, such as the Pacific Plate, move faster than those predominantly composed of continental lithosphere, such as the Eurasian Plate.

PINGVELLIR FAULT

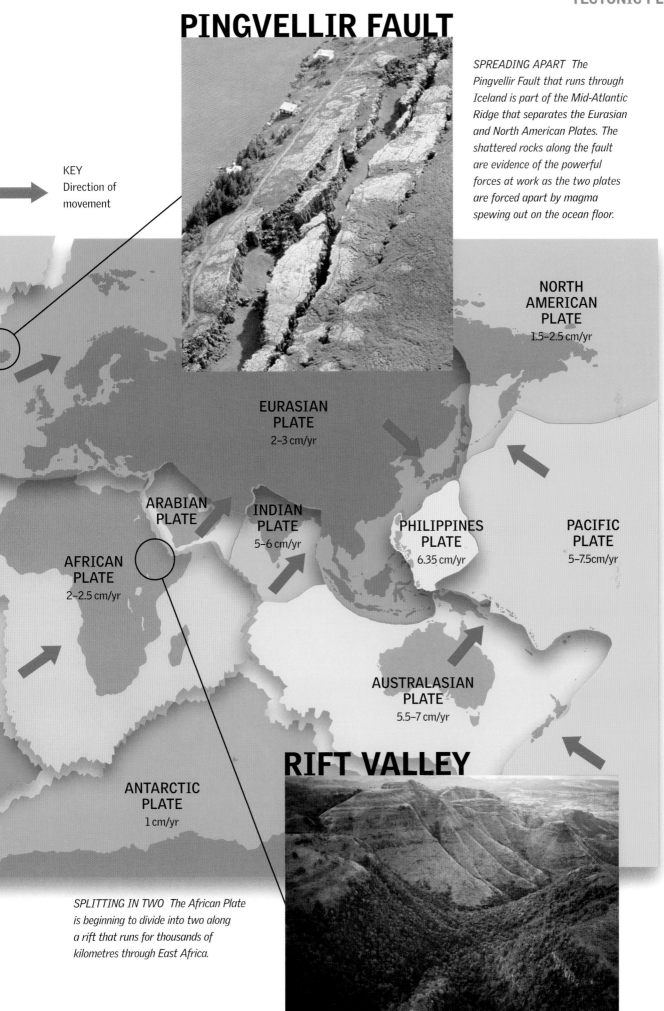

SPREADING APART The Pingvellir Fault that runs through Iceland is part of the Mid-Atlantic Ridge that separates the Eurasian and North American Plates. The shattered rocks along the fault are evidence of the powerful forces at work as the two plates are forced apart by magma spewing out on the ocean floor.

KEY
Direction of
movement

NORTH
AMERICAN
PLATE
1.5–2.5 cm/yr

EURASIAN
PLATE
2–3 cm/yr

ARABIAN
PLATE

INDIAN
PLATE
5–6 cm/yr

PHILIPPINES
PLATE
6.35 cm/yr

PACIFIC
PLATE
5–7.5cm/yr

AFRICAN
PLATE
2–2.5 cm/yr

AUSTRALASIAN
PLATE
5.5–7 cm/yr

ANTARCTIC
PLATE
1 cm/yr

RIFT VALLEY

SPLITTING IN TWO The African Plate is beginning to divide into two along a rift that runs for thousands of kilometres through East Africa.

PLATE BOUNDARIES

A HIGH PROPORTION OF THE ENERGY THAT IS RELEASED AT THE EARTH'S SURFACE in the form of earthquakes and volcanic activity occurs at the boundaries between tectonic plates. Scientists have studied these plate boundaries intensively in their quest to understand the processes that lead to earthquakes and volcanic eruptions. They have grouped boundaries into three main types: divergent or constructive boundaries (where two plates are moving apart); convergent boundaries (where two plates are moving towards each other); and transform boundaries (where the edges of two plates slide past each other).

VOLCANIC ISLANDS The subduction of the Pacific Plate's western edge under several neighbouring plates has led to the creation of strings of volcanic islands, such as the Kuril Islands.

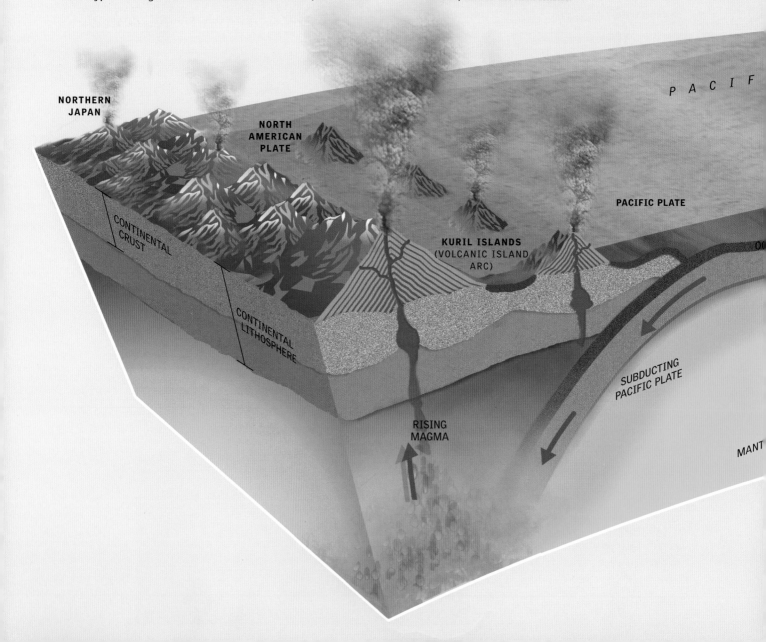

NORTHERN JAPAN

NORTH AMERICAN PLATE

PACIFIC PLATE

P A C I F

CONTINENTAL CRUST

CONTINENTAL LITHOSPHERE

KURIL ISLANDS (VOLCANIC ISLAND ARC)

OC

SUBDUCTING PACIFIC PLATE

RISING MAGMA

MANT

DIVERGING PLATES The East Pacific Rise is a mid-ocean ridge, a divergent boundary between the Nazca and Pacific oceanic plates. As new lithosphere is created, the two plates move away from it at about 5–10 cm a year. At their far edges, the plates are subducted (slide down) beneath the edges of neighbouring plates.

PUSHING UP THE ANDES
The subduction of the Nazca Plate under the South American Plate has contributed to the creation of the Andean mountain chain and volcanoes.

ISLAND HOTSPOTS
The chain of volcanic islands we know as Hawaii (see the satellite image, top) was created over tens of millions of years as the Pacific Plate moved slowly over a hotspot – a plume of hot magma rising up from the Earth's mantle.

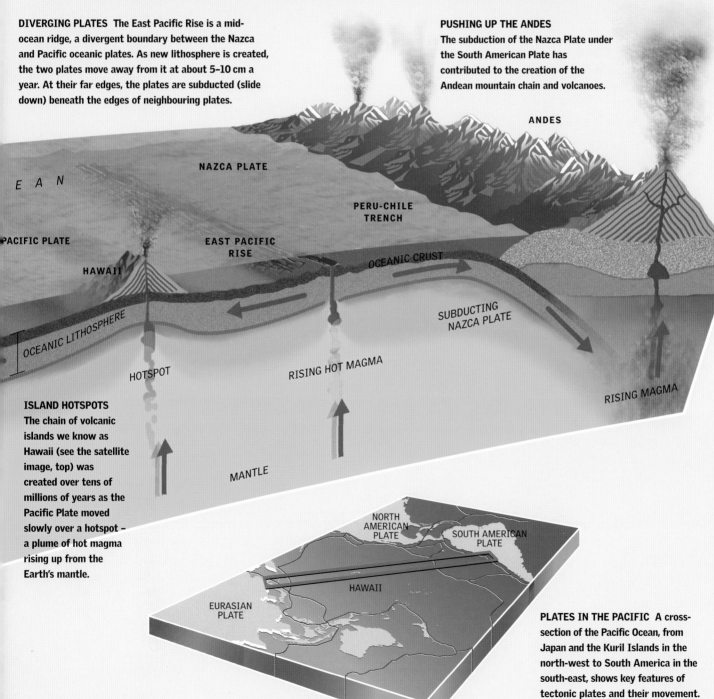

ANDES

NAZCA PLATE

PERU-CHILE
TRENCH

E A N

PACIFIC PLATE

EAST PACIFIC
RISE

HAWAII

OCEANIC CRUST

OCEANIC LITHOSPHERE

SUBDUCTING
NAZCA PLATE

HOTSPOT

RISING HOT MAGMA

RISING MAGMA

MANTLE

NORTH
AMERICAN
PLATE

SOUTH AMERICAN
PLATE

HAWAII

EURASIAN
PLATE

PLATES IN THE PACIFIC A cross-section of the Pacific Ocean, from Japan and the Kuril Islands in the north-west to South America in the south-east, shows key features of tectonic plates and their movement.

DIVERGENT BOUNDARIES

THE MOST EXTENSIVE DIVERGENT PLATE BOUNDARIES ON EARTH ARE THE MID-OCEAN SPREADING RIDGES. These snake across the bottoms of the world's oceans like vast interconnected chains of underwater volcanoes. The ridge system – which includes the Mid-Atlantic Ridge, the East Pacific Rise and other ridges in the Indian and Southern Oceans – extends for about 65 000 km. It is the largest single volcanic feature on Earth – in fact, it is the largest single geological feature on the Earth's surface.

The ridges develop at plate boundaries where new lithosphere (see page 20) is continuously formed from magma (molten rock) that is welling up from the mantle below. The magma beneath a spreading ridge typically collects in a reservoir lying a few kilometres underground. Some of it eventually solidifies in place within the lithosphere, forming the bulk of the new oceanic crust. Some, however, forces its way out onto the sea floor, via a system of dykes and fissures.

Scientists recognise two types of ridge. Slow-spreading ridges, like the Mid-Atlantic Ridge, form new lithosphere at a rate of about 2–5 cm a year – they have deep depressions or valleys running down their centres. Fast-spreading ridges, which include the East Pacific Rise, create new lithosphere at 10–20 cm a year

RIFT VALLEY A continental rift develops when an upwelling of magma into the lithosphere stretches a section of continental crust above it. Fissures appear in the crust, and volcanoes emerge. Eventually, the land sinks to form a rift valley, which contains volcanoes and volcanic fissures.

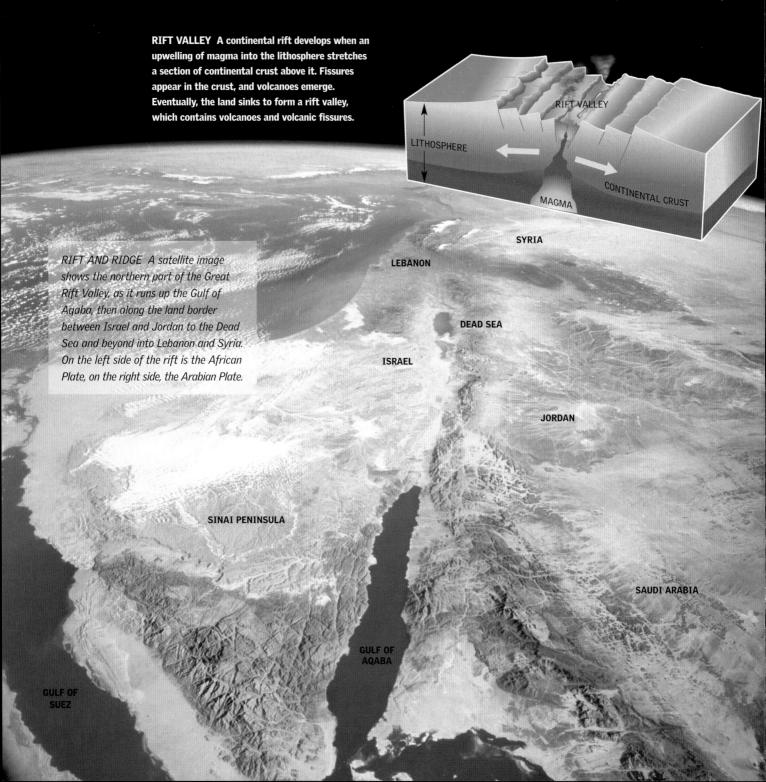

RIFT AND RIDGE A satellite image shows the northern part of the Great Rift Valley, as it runs up the Gulf of Aqaba, then along the land border between Israel and Jordan to the Dead Sea and beyond into Lebanon and Syria. On the left side of the rift is the African Plate, on the right side, the Arabian Plate.

and lack a central valley. Earthquakes often occur at mid-ocean ridges, but they are shallow and generally of small magnitude.

Another type of divergent plate boundary appears in the middle of a landmass. Rift valleys or continental rift zones occur where particularly large plumes of magma rise up from the mantle under a landmass, causing the lithosphere to soften, weaken, stretch and thin out. Eventually, long linear faults appear in the continental crust, typically in three different directions.

Sinking land

Initially, no new lithosphere is created along these rift faults. Instead, land sinks along the faults, and a series of volcanoes develops in the fault zone as magma reaches the surface. In due course, along at least two of the three faults, the land starts moving apart, sea floods in to fill the gaps and new mid-ocean ridges develop at the bottom of the sea. These start creating new lithosphere, pushing apart the chunks of land that were once joined.

The best-known example of a rift boundary is the Great Rift Valley, which runs for 6300 km from Syria, through the Jordan Valley, the Gulf of Aqaba and the Red Sea and into East Africa, where it extends south from Eritrea to Mozambique. In the Red Sea and Gulf of Aqaba, the land has already split apart along the boundary between the African and Arabian Plates and the sea has flooded in. The part of the rift valley that extends through Africa, called the East African rift zone, is regarded as a developing, rather than a fully fledged, plate boundary. It contains numerous active volcanoes (see pages 82-83) and is expected eventually to split the Horn of Africa from the rest of the continent.

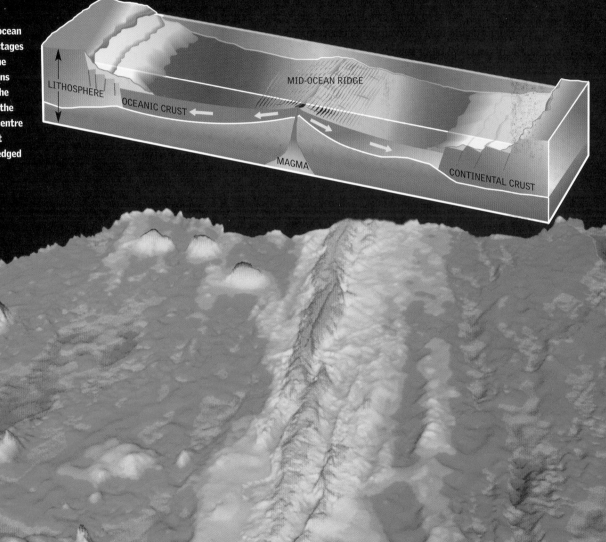

MID-OCEAN RIDGE A mid-ocean spreading ridge develops in stages from a continental rift. As the continental crust in a rift thins and the rift valley extends, the ocean eventually floods into the rift. On the sea floor at the centre of the rift, new oceanic crust begins to form and a fully fledged mid-ocean ridge develops.

LITHOSPHERE

OCEANIC CRUST

MID-OCEAN RIDGE

MAGMA

CONTINENTAL CRUST

PACIFIC DEPTHS
A sonar image shows
the rugged contours
of a section of the
East Pacific Rise.

VOLCANIC ARC The numerous volcanoes along Russia's Kamchatka Peninsula are arranged along an arc at an ocean–continent convergent plate boundary. They result from the Pacific Plate being subducted beneath a part of the North American Plate.

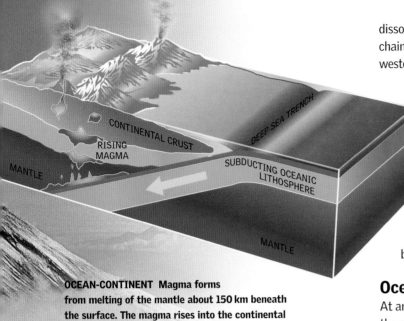

OCEAN-CONTINENT Magma forms from melting of the mantle about 150 km beneath the surface. The magma rises into the continental crust by melting the rock above it. Magma chambers form around 5–10 km below the surface, and from there the magma can well upwards via pipes and conduits to the vents of volcanoes.

CONVERGENT BOUNDARIES

CONVERGENT BOUNDARIES FALL INTO THREE TYPES, DEPENDING ON WHETHER THE EDGES OF THE PLATES MEETING AT THE BOUNDARY contain different types of crust (ocean-continent) or the same kind (ocean-ocean and continent-continent). In all cases, they are major sites of earthquakes, and all but the continent-continent boundaries are common sites of volcanic eruptions.

Ocean-continent boundaries

At an ocean-continent boundary, the edge of a plate of oceanic lithosphere subducts (slides down) beneath a thick slab of continental lithosphere. Along the boundary, a deep trench usually forms in the ocean floor. An example can be found off the west coast of South America, where the edge of the oceanic Nazca Plate is subducting beneath the continental lithosphere of the South American Plate. A similar subduction exists along part of the west coast of North America.

One effect of a plate subducting under a continent is that it lifts up the overriding plate, creating a mountain chain – in the case of South America, the Andes. As the subducting plate descends, its temperature rises, driving off volatile substances, such as water, that were trapped in the oceanic crust. As this water enters the mantle of the overriding plate, it lowers the melting temperature of the surrounding mantle, producing magma that contains large amounts of

dissolved gases. These 'melts' rise to the surface, forming long chains of volcanoes inland from the continental shelf – along the western parts of South America, these volcanoes are interspersed within the mountains that form the rest of the Andes. Because of its high volume of extremely pressurised gases, this magma contributes to some of the most explosive volcanoes on Earth.

A further effect is that, although the subducting plate mostly sinks down smoothly and continuously, its deepest parts break into smaller pieces. These become locked in place for long periods of time before suddenly moving to generate large earthquakes. Such earthquakes are often accompanied by uplift of the overlying land by as much as a few metres.

Ocean-ocean boundaries

At an ocean-ocean boundary, the subducting plate is normally the one whose edge is composed of older lithosphere, because as oceanic lithosphere ages, it becomes colder, denser and heavier. A deep trench develops, and magma forms in the region above the subducting plate. But instead of forming a series of volcanoes that intermingle with surrounding mountains, the rising magma at an ocean-ocean boundary typically forms an arc of volcanoes that rise out of the ocean as islands. An example is the Sunda volcanic arc of Indonesia, caused by subduction of the Australasian Plate under the Eurasian Plate. In some cases, the individual volcanoes in an arc have coalesced to form large islands, such as the island of Java in the Sunda arc.

Ocean-ocean convergence zones are frequently affected by earthquakes. A massive one near the Sunda arc caused the December 26, 2004, Indian Ocean tsunami.

Continent-continent boundaries

If the edges of two colliding plates both carry continental crust, neither fully subducts under the other. This is because continental crust has a relatively low density and so usually resists downward

OCEAN-OCEAN Magma forms from the melting of the mantle at a depth of 100–120 km. An arc of volcanic islands develops, typically running parallel to the submarine trench marking the boundary between the plates.

motion. Instead, the crust on either side of the boundary is compressed and subjected to high temperatures and pressures. As a result, the crustal rocks are folded and faulted, and the underlying lithosphere thickens. A huge amount of uplift is generated, pushing the continental crust high into the sky. One such collision started around 50 million years ago when plate movements drove India into Asia. Following the collision, the Eurasian Plate crumpled up and overrode the Indian Plate. The slow convergence of the two plates over millions of years pushed the Himalayas and the Tibetan Plateau to their present heights. Elsewhere, continent-continent collisions have pushed up ranges such as the European Alps and the High Atlas of North Africa.

At these boundaries, some magma is produced where the lithosphere of one plate is partially subducted under the neighbouring plate. This magma is trapped at a depth of around 200 km beneath a massive plug of continental crust, so it rarely reaches anywhere near the surface. Earthquakes are common, but volcanic activity at these boundaries is usually rare.

CONTINENT-CONTINENT Enormous forces are exerted on the rocks where the two plates meet, causing the crust to crumple, fold, deform, compress and alter its chemical composition. Some of the rock is pushed skywards to form the peaks of mountains, while other rock is pushed down to form their 'roots'.

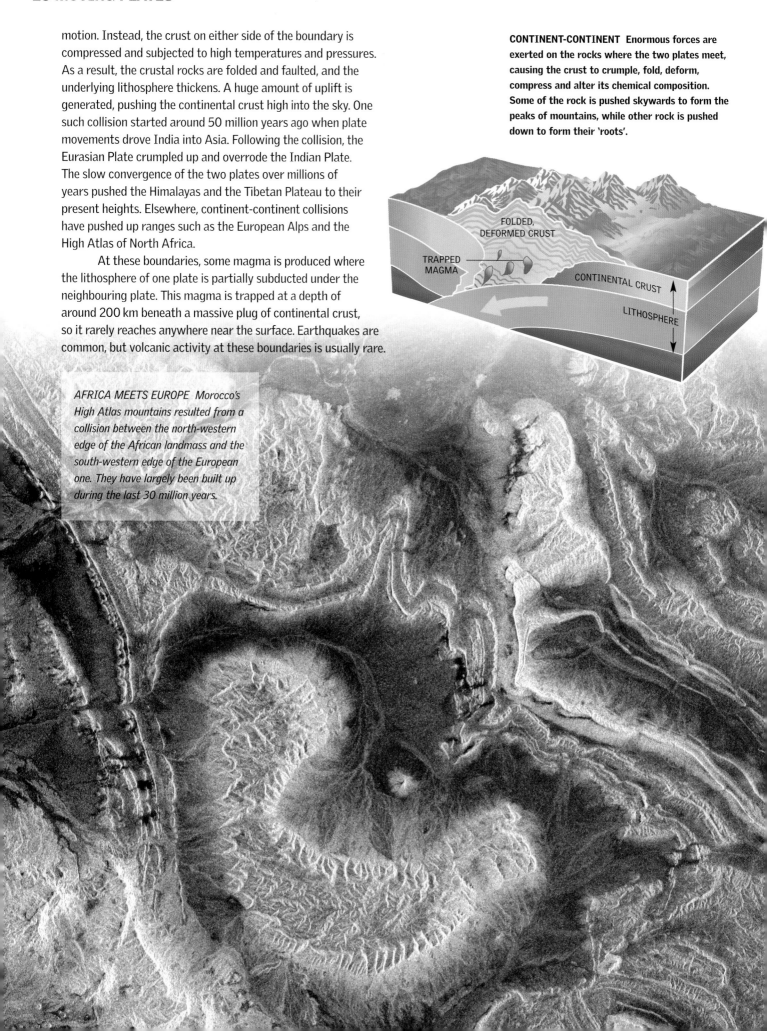

FOLDED, DEFORMED CRUST

TRAPPED MAGMA

CONTINENTAL CRUST

LITHOSPHERE

AFRICA MEETS EUROPE Morocco's High Atlas mountains resulted from a collision between the north-western edge of the African landmass and the south-western edge of the European one. They have largely been built up during the last 30 million years.

TRANSFORM BOUNDARIES

A ZONE WHERE TWO PLATES SLIDE HORIZONTALLY PAST EACH OTHER IS CALLED A TRANSFORM-FAULT BOUNDARY OR SIMPLY A TRANSFORM BOUNDARY. Canadian geophysicist John Tuzo Wilson first formulated the idea of transform faults in the 1960s. He proposed that these large faults connect two divergent plate boundaries or, less commonly, convergent boundaries. Most transform faults – which are also called fracture zones – are found on the ocean floor, where they offset the active mid-ocean spreading ridges, producing zigzag plate margins. Along the Mid-Atlantic Ridge, for example, fracture zones occur at an average interval of 55 km. Along the fracture zones, short sections of plate move past each other in different directions.

Although most transform fault boundaries are submarine, a few occur on land. One example is the Alpine Fault on New Zealand's South Island, where the Australasian Plate grinds past the Pacific Plate, but the best known specimen is the San Andreas Fault in California. This connects the East Pacific Rise – the main mid-ocean ridge in the south-eastern and central eastern Pacific Ocean – to other spreading ridges in the north-eastern Pacific. Earthquakes, including the famous San Francisco earthquake of 1906, occur regularly at different points along the fault. The San Andreas is the most extensively studied earthquake fault zone on Earth.

SAN ANDREAS FAULT Along the San Andreas Fault, which slices for more than 1300 km through California, the Pacific Plate has ground past the North American Plate for 10 million years, at an average rate of about 5 cm per year. Land on the Pacific Plate is moving in a north-westerly direction relative to the land on the North American Plate.

SIDE BY SIDE At a transform boundary, two plates slide past each other. Lithosphere is neither created nor destroyed, but as sections of plate grind past each other, they often become 'locked', so that no movement occurs for years. When movement does happen, there can be a large release of energy in an earthquake.

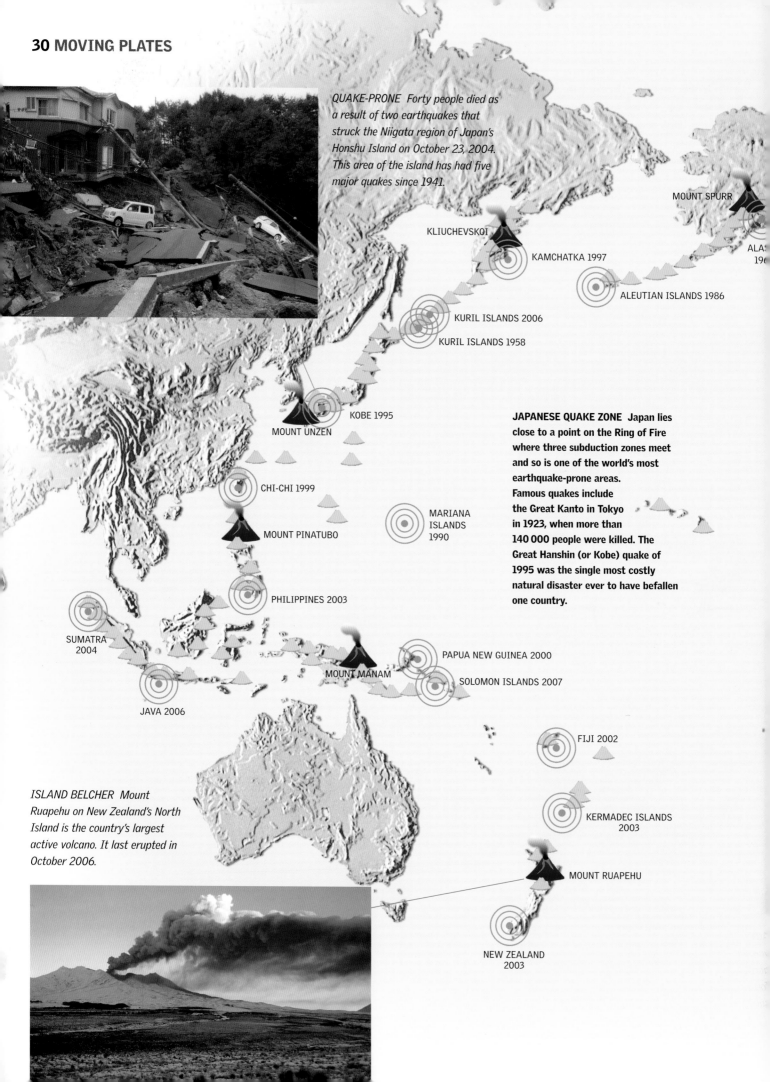

QUAKE-PRONE Forty people died as a result of two earthquakes that struck the Niigata region of Japan's Honshu Island on October 23, 2004. This area of the island has had five major quakes since 1941.

KLIUCHEVSKOI

KAMCHATKA 1997

MOUNT SPURR

ALAS 196

ALEUTIAN ISLANDS 1986

KURIL ISLANDS 2006

KURIL ISLANDS 1958

KOBE 1995

MOUNT UNZEN

JAPANESE QUAKE ZONE Japan lies close to a point on the Ring of Fire where three subduction zones meet and so is one of the world's most earthquake-prone areas. Famous quakes include the Great Kanto in Tokyo in 1923, when more than 140 000 people were killed. The Great Hanshin (or Kobe) quake of 1995 was the single most costly natural disaster ever to have befallen one country.

CHI-CHI 1999

MARIANA ISLANDS 1990

MOUNT PINATUBO

PHILIPPINES 2003

SUMATRA 2004

MOUNT MANAM

PAPUA NEW GUINEA 2000

SOLOMON ISLANDS 2007

JAVA 2006

FIJI 2002

ISLAND BELCHER Mount Ruapehu on New Zealand's North Island is the country's largest active volcano. It last erupted in October 2006.

KERMADEC ISLANDS 2003

MOUNT RUAPEHU

NEW ZEALAND 2003

KEY

Notably active volcanoes since 1980

Active volcanoes

Major earthquakes since 1955

MOUNT ST HELENS

LOS ANGELES 1944

COLIMA

MEXICO 1985

ARENAL

GUATEMALA 1976

NEVADO DEL RUIZ

GALERAS

ECUADOR 1998

PERU 1970

SABANCAYA

CHILE 1960

VILLARRICA

ACTIVE ARENAL This Costa Rican volcano has been almost constantly active since 1968. It is one of many formed where the Cocos Plate subducts under the Caribbean Plate.

RING OF FIRE

AROUND 80 PER CENT OF THE WORLD'S LARGER EARTHQUAKES and 70 per cent of its active and dormant volcanoes above sea level occur on the Pacific Ring of Fire. Earthquakes in the Ring of Fire over the past 50 years have included the Kobe quake in Japan in 1995 and other massive ones off Chile (in 1960), near Mexico City (1985) and the Solomon Islands (2007). Some of the larger volcanic eruptions have included those of Mount St Helens in 1980 and Mount Pinatubo in the Philippines (1991).

About 40 000 km in length, the Ring of Fire almost completely encircles the Pacific Ocean. In addition to volcanoes, it includes areas of geothermal activity, notably on the North Island of New Zealand and in Japan, Russia's Kamchatka Peninsula, the western United States and Chile.

A jigsaw of plates

The Ring of Fire was recognised and described long before anything was known about tectonic plates. Once the tectonic theory had been developed, the distribution of earthquakes and volcanoes around the Pacific made sense. Each section of the Ring of Fire lies on a convergent plate boundary – in nearly all cases an area where one of the main plates of the Pacific dips beneath a neighbouring plate.

On the eastern side of the Pacific, the Nazca and Cocos Plates are subducted beneath the South American and Caribbean Plates, while a portion of the Pacific Plate and the small Juan de Fuca Plate slide below the North American Plate. In the northern Pacific, the Pacific Plate, moving north-westwards, is subducted beneath the arc of the Aleutian Islands, while in the north-west it slips beneath part of the North American Plate along the Kamchatka and Kuril Islands volcanic arc and part of Japan.

Farther south, the Pacific Plate dips beneath the Philippines Plate, which is itself subducted under the Eurasian Plate – these interactions have created the southern part of Japan, the Philippines and the Mariana Islands, all of them volcanically active. The final section of the Ring of Fire runs from New Guinea through parts of Melanesia as far as New Zealand. Along a large part of this section, the Pacific Plate slides under the Australasian Plate.

MEASURING PLATE MOVEMENTS

SCIENTISTS HAVE DEVELOPED A NUMBER OF WAYS TO WORK OUT HOW FAST THE EARTH'S PLATES ARE MOVING. These include the use of laser light, the Global Positioning System (GPS) and radiotelescopes. Satellite Laser Ranging (SLR) relies on short bursts of laser light sent from ground stations on different plates to orbiting satellites and reflected back to the ground stations. By precise measurement of the travel times, the distance between the ground stations can be calculated. By repeating the measurements every few years, the plate movements can be worked out.

A similar approach uses GPS satellites. Twenty-one of these satellites are in orbit above the Earth, continuously transmitting radio signals. By simultaneously receiving signals from at least four satellites, a GPS ground receiver can determine its precise longitude, latitude and elevation on Earth. By repeatedly comparing the distances between two fixed receivers, scientists can determine the relative movements of the plates on which the receivers are positioned. Very Long Baseline Interferometry (see right) uses radiotelescopes to measure plate movements.

Past movements

Measuring plate movements can also be extended into the past. One way is to analyse the magnetic properties of rocks at the bottom of the oceans (see box, above). No sea-floor rock is older than about 150 million years, so for clues about how the Earth's plates moved before that time, scientists study continental rocks. As plate movements have rotated the continents over the millennia, the ancient rocks have turned with them, and where the magnetic minerals in those rocks once pointed north they now point somewhere else. By plotting these shifts, scientists can calculate how the continents have moved.

Another method is to study chains of islands that form as plates pass over hotspots in the Earth's mantle (see pages 96-97). Research into the Hawaiian island chain, for example, has shown that for the past 43 million years the Pacific Plate has been moving in a north-westerly direction at a rate of about 7 cm a year. Another method is based on the idea that continents such as South America and Africa were once joined together. By examining the shapes of their boundaries and the geological structures and fossils near them, scientists can work out how they once fitted together and what plate movements brought the continents to their current configuration.

MAGNETIC PATTERNS

When oceanic crust forms from volcanic material at mid-ocean spreading ridges (see page 22), the Earth's magnetic field gives the rock a particular magnetic 'signature', depending on the magnetic field's strength and direction at the time the crust forms. From time to time, the magnetic field reverses direction, and this is recorded in the sea-floor rock. As a result, the sea floor has a striped pattern of magnetisation, rather like a retail bar code. The differences are slight, but sensitive magnetometers can detect them. Because scientists know the dates of all the magnetic reversals, magnetic maps of the sea floor can be translated into age maps – and in this way they can ascertain the rates at which plates have moved away from mid-ocean ridges.

SPLIT FIELD The Nojima Fault, which slices across Japan's Awaji Island, is part of the fault system involved in the Kobe earthquake of 1995. It is clearly visible here as it cuts across a farmer's field – a constant reminder of the forces at work where the Earth's tectonic plates meet.

MEASURING MOVEMENT BY RADIOTELESCOPE In Very Long Baseline Interferometry (VLBI), two telescopes sited on different plates are pointed at a quasar – a distant object in the Universe that emits natural radio waves. Using atomic clocks, scientists measure the times when particular radio signals from the quasar reach each telescope. From the time differences, they calculate the distance between the telescopes. By repeating the exercise every few years, they can work out the relative movement of the telescopes from each other, and hence of the plates on which they are positioned.

PLATES AND EVOLUTION

THE SHIFTING OF THE EARTH'S CONTINENTS HAS HAD A DRAMATIC INFLUENCE ON THE EVOLUTION AND DISTRIBUTION OF LIFE. Modern discoveries about 'continental drift' explain how the break-up of landmasses split some species into isolated groups, which later evolved in separate ways. Where continents joined together, this encouraged the spread of newly evolved organisms.

People have speculated for centuries that the positions of the continents were different in the past from what they are today. As early as the 16th century, geographers noted that the shapes of the continents on either side of the Atlantic seemed to fit together. Then, in the late 19th century, geologists noticed that fossils and geological formations from different southern hemisphere continents showed remarkable similarities.

In 1912, a German scientist, Alfred Wegener, published his theory of continental drift, drawing together evidence to show that South America had once been joined to Africa, and Europe to North America. He was unable, however, to provide any convincing explanation for the physical processes involved. His theory was not taken seriously until 1928, when a geologist called Arthur Holmes proposed that heat convection in the Earth's mantle might provide a mechanism for moving the continents. In 1962, US geologist Harry Hess suggested that continents are attached to ocean floors, and that both continents and ocean floor move over the Earth's mantle, driven by heat convection. Within ten years, the theory of plate tectonics was accepted by most Earth scientists.

Marsupials and placentals

One example of how these processes affected evolution involves the two main groups of mammals – marsupials and placentals. Scientists believe that around 200 million years ago nearly all of the Earth's land was united in a single continent, Pangaea. Then, around 180 million years ago, this started breaking apart into a northern continent, Laurasia, containing what is now North America, Europe and Asia – but not India – and a southern one, Gondwana, which contained all the rest of the land. For a considerable time, a land bridge persisted between the two.

About 140 million years ago, Gondwana started breaking up into three pieces, corresponding to South America-Africa, India and Antarctica-Australia. Over the next 20 million years, the first marsupial mammals evolved, probably in Laurasia, and spread across the land bridge into Gondwana. From South America, they crossed to Antarctica-Australia via another land bridge.

By about 100 million years ago, South America and Africa had split and placental mammals had evolved on Laurasia. They later spread to South America, Africa and India, when these crashed into Laurasia or became linked to it by land bridges, and largely displaced the marsupials there. They never reached Antarctica-Australia, however, which had already disconnected from the other continents. Then, about 50 million years ago, Australia and Antarctica split. Antarctica shifted to the South Pole, where conditions were too cold for its marsupials to survive. Australia moved north, and with no competition from the placentals, its marsupials thrived.

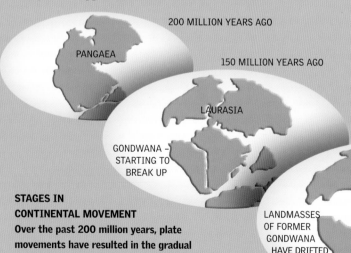

STAGES IN CONTINENTAL MOVEMENT
Over the past 200 million years, plate movements have resulted in the gradual redistribution of the Earth's continental landmasses. These maps show four stages along the way, from the break-up of the original continent of Pangaea to the emergence of a world map similar to the one we know today.

200 MILLION YEARS AGO

PANGAEA

150 MILLION YEARS AGO

LAURASIA

GONDWANA – STARTING TO BREAK UP

LAURASIA HAS SPLIT

LANDMASSES OF FORMER GONDWANA HAVE DRIFTED APART

3 MILLION YEARS AGO

NORTH AND SOUTH AMERICA HAVE JOINED

INDIA HAS JOINED EURASIAN LANDMASS

65 MILLION YEARS AGO

MARSUPIAL SURVIVORS A termite-eating numbat is one of the many marsupials that thrived in Australia, isolated from the rest of the world as a result of continental drift. Elsewhere, marsupials lost out to competition from placental mammals.

FOSSIL LEAF EVIDENCE Similar tongue-shaped fossilised leaves have been found in rock strata in different continents. They come from an extinct shrub called Glossopteris. Findings such as these caused 19th-century scientists to speculate that the southern continents must once have been joined in a single giant continent.

AFRICA

ANTARCTICA

AUSTRALIA

SOUTH AMERICA

INDIA

SHAK
EA

ING
RTH

2

CARS ARE SANDWICHED AND SMASHED
BETWEEN SECTIONS OF THE SAN
FRANCISCO BAY BRIDGE, WHICH
COLLAPSED DURING AN EARTHQUAKE
IN 1989. Earthquakes strong enough to cause
this scale of devastation rank among the most
terrifying expressions of Earth's power and
explosive energy. Triggered by sudden
movements in the Earth's crust, large
earthquakes can have a devastating effect on
buildings and other structures, they can set off
fires or deadly tsunamis and, in the worst
cases, claim hundreds of thousands of lives.
Over the past 4000 years, some 13 million
people are known to have died as a result of
major earthquakes. Despite advances in
monitoring techniques, earthquakes cannot be
predicted with any certainty, and will continue
to take an enormous human and economic toll.

CAUSES OF QUAKES

AS THE TECTONIC PLATES THAT MAKE UP THE EARTH'S CRUST GRIND PAST EACH OTHER, THEY GENERATE ENORMOUS FRICTIONAL STRESS. Instead of gliding past each other smoothly, the huge slabs of rock move in a series of sudden jerks and judders. In certain regions along plate boundaries, opposing masses of rock sometimes reach a stalemate where they become locked together. While the blocks of rock are unable to move further, the powerful forces behind overall plate movement cause a gradual build-up of pressure, called strain energy. Eventually, the pressure becomes so great it overcomes the resistance of the blockage, producing a sudden shift between the blocks of rock. As these give way, the strain energy is released in shock or seismic waves.

Creep versus quake

Usually the amount of energy released with each shift is small and is known as creep. It is rare for an area undergoing creep to experience a large earthquake because the stress is continually being relieved. But sometimes two blocks of lithosphere become locked together for decades, or even centuries. The rocks accumulate a huge level of strain energy, becoming compressed and deformed in the process. When the failure eventually occurs,

ALASKA
1964

SAN FRANCISCO
1906

MEXICO CITY
1985

SOUTH PE
2001

CHIL
196

WASHED AWAY The most powerful earthquake ever recorded in North America struck a southern coastal region of Alaska on Good Friday, March 27, 1964, with a magnitude 9.2. It demolished hundreds of buildings and in places caused the land to rise or sink by up to 11 m.

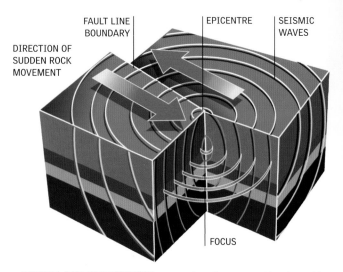

DIRECTION OF
SUDDEN ROCK
MOVEMENT

FAULT LINE
BOUNDARY

EPICENTRE

SEISMIC
WAVES

FOCUS

INSIDE AN EARTHQUAKE An earthquake is caused by the sudden rupture of a region of stressed rock. Waves of energy (seismic waves) emanate from a spot underground called the earthquake focus. The site on Earth's surface located directly above the focus is called the epicentre.

EARTHQUAKE ZONES The map highlights (in pink) the regions most prone to earthquakes. There are two major zones: one stretching from Indonesia to the Mediterranean, and the other encircling the Pacific Ocean (the Ring of Fire). Mid-ocean ridges are also earthquake-prone. Also shown are the locations of 16 of the most powerful earthquakes since 1900.

RUINED CITY The quake in Kashmir in 2005 killed 73 000 people, many of them in the city of Balakot as a result of building collapse.

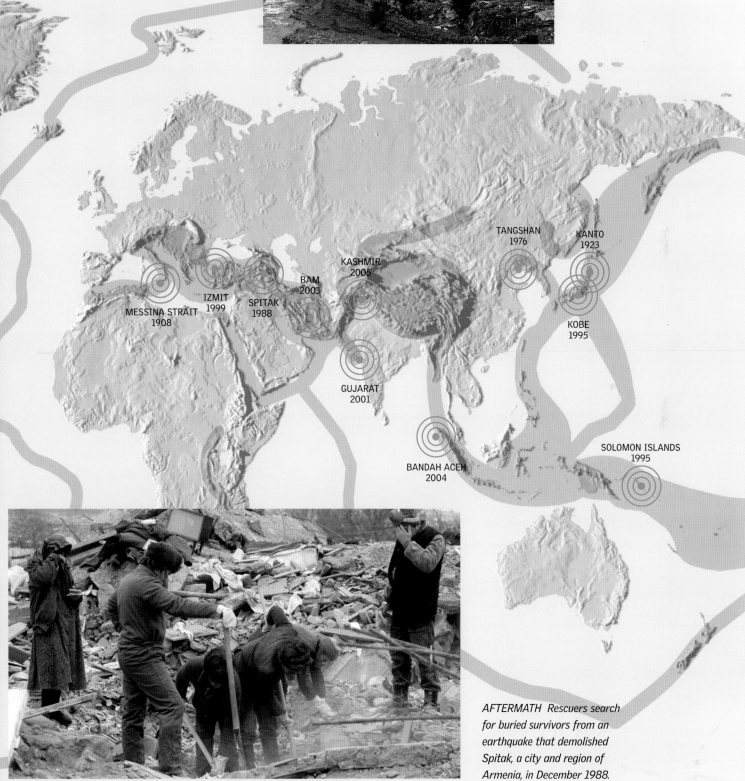

TANGSHAN
1976

KANTO
1923

KASHMIR
2005

BAM
2003

IZMIT
1999

SPITAK
1988

MESSINA STRAIT
1908

KOBE
1995

GUJARAT
2001

BANDAH ACEH
2004

SOLOMON ISLANDS
1995

AFTERMATH Rescuers search for buried survivors from an earthquake that demolished Spitak, a city and region of Armenia, in December 1988.

it can cause a large shift of several metres with a corresponding colossal release of energy. In some cases, the energy release is so massive that the whole planet wobbles slightly on its axis.

Types of earthquake

Earthquakes are grouped into three categories based on depth. Shallow-focus quakes have a focus less than 70 km deep. These are the most destructive quakes because they are near the surface, where rocks are stronger and so can build up more strain energy before they fail. Intermediate-focus quakes have centres at depths of 70–300 km, while deep-focus earthquakes have a focus more than 300 km deep.

Earthquakes occur along fault planes, which often coincide with, or are parallel and close to, plate boundaries. Strike-slip faults typically occur at transform plate boundaries, where two blocks of lithosphere are grinding past each other side by side. Thrust faults happen at convergent boundaries, where one plate dives beneath the other. Normal faults occur at divergent boundaries; in these, one block of lithosphere drops down and away from the other.

Where earthquakes occur

Over 95 per cent of earthquakes happen at convergent plate boundaries – about 80 per cent of them on the Pacific 'Ring of Fire' (see pages 30–31). The next most common sites are transform boundaries, such as the boundary between the Pacific Plate and the North American Plate that runs through California.

REDUCED TO RUBBLE A residential area of Izmit in north-western Turkey lies in ruins after an earthquake hit the city in August 1999.

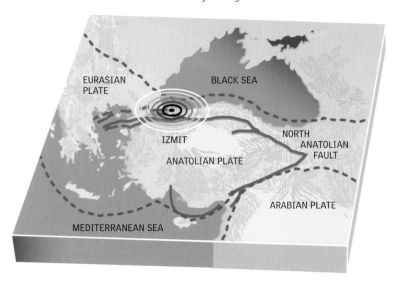

NORTH ANATOLIAN FAULT Izmit sits on the North Anatolian fault in northern Turkey. Over the past 70 years, a series of earthquakes (sometimes referred to as an earthquake storm) has occurred along this fault as the small Anatolian Plate has moved westwards relative to the Eurasian Plate. Some experts think that the next major quake may strike near Istanbul, to the west of Izmit.

DETECTION AND MEASUREMENT

HOW DO SCIENTISTS MEASURE THE INTENSITY OF AN EARTHQUAKE? Quakes are often described by their magnitudes, reported as a number on the Richter scale. An earthquake's magnitude is worked out from a recording, or seismogram, made by a seismometer of the waves that emanate from the earthquake's focus. These waves travel through the Earth's interior and are picked up by a network of seismometers around the globe. Scientists calculate the distance of the individual seismometers from the quake, and from this information they can pinpoint the exact location of an earthquake's focus and its magnitude.

Locating an earthquake – tracking the waves

During an earthquake, two main types of waves emanate from the quake's focus: surface waves and body waves. Surface waves travel within the Earth's crust and are responsible for most of the destruction associated with an earthquake. Body waves – primary or P waves and secondary or S waves – travel through Earth's interior.

P waves travel slightly faster than S waves, and this fact enables scientists to locate the focus of an earthquake. When a quake occurs, monitoring stations pick up the difference in the arrival times of the first P wave and the first S wave. From this, scientists at each station work out their distance from the quake focus. Each one then plots a circle using their distance from the focus as the radius. When three circles from different stations intercept, the point of interception gives the location of the epicentre.

In the case of earthquakes in more remote parts of the world, the detection of four or more P-wave arrivals at different monitoring stations permits seismologists to calculate the location of an earthquake and its timing. In practice, dozens or even hundreds of P-wave arrivals are used.

Magnitude

Once scientists have identified the location and time of an earthquake, they use this information together with the height, or amplitude, of the strongest wave to determine the earthquake's magnitude. The Richter scale is often used to describe an earthquake's magnitude, but it is just one of several scales. To describe particularly large earthquakes, seismologists generally prefer to use the moment magnitude scale, because this gives a more precise estimate of the quake's

PATHS OF BODY WAVES When an earthquake occurs, seismic waves race outwards in all directions. The P (shown in blue) and S (white) waves travel through the Earth's interior at different speeds – only P waves can travel through the core. Monitoring stations work out their distance from the earthquake focus from the time difference between the first P and S waves to arrive. This information from several monitoring stations is combined to determine the exact location and magnitude of the earthquake. Analysis of the waves has also told scientists a great deal about the make-up of the Earth's interior.

S AND P WAVES DETECTED

S AND P WAVES DETECTED

S AND P WAVES DETECTED

S AND P WAVES DETECTED

P WAVES DETECTED

EPICENTRE

P WAVES DETECTED

S AND P WAVES DETECTED

P WAVES DETECTED

S AND P WAVES DETECTED

S AND P WAVES DETECTED

MODIFIED MERCALLI SCALE

This scale describes the intensity of an earthquake in terms of its effects. A quake is rated after inspecting the damage and interviewing survivors.

 1 Only detectable by instruments.

 2 A few people might notice a slight movement if they are at rest and/or on the upper floors of buildings.

 3 Many people indoors feel movement like the passing of a truck. Hanging objects swing back and forth.

 4 Most people indoors feel movement. Dishes, windows and doors rattle. A few people outdoors may feel it. Parked cars rock.

 5 Almost everyone feels movement. Dishes are broken, sleeping people are woken up. Liquids spill out of open containers.

 6 Felt by all. Objects fall from shelves and pictures fall off walls. Plaster may crack and furniture moves.

 7 Noticed by people in cars. Loose tiles fall from roofs. Considerable damage occurs in poorly constructed buildings.

 8 Standing upright becomes extremely difficult. Houses may shift on their foundations. Chimneys and monuments twist and fall.

 9 Great damage to substantial structures, including bridges and roads. Large cracks appear. Underground pipes break.

 10 Disastrous degree of damage. Most buildings destroyed, including earthquake-resistant structures. Dams seriously damaged.

 11 Few structures left standing. Underground pipes destroyed, railway tracks badly bent.

 12 Catastrophic, total destruction. Waves travel visibly along the ground surface and throw large objects into the air.

---

size. For most earthquakes, the difference between Richter magnitude and moment magnitude is significant but not great – for example, a large earthquake near Northridge, California, in 1994 had a Richter magnitude of 6.7 and a moment magnitude of 6.4. In both the Richter and moment magnitude scales, a 1-point increase on the scale represents roughly a 32-fold increase in the energy released. So there is a huge difference between, say, an earthquake of magnitude 5 and one of magnitude 8 – the latter releases about 32 000 times more energy.

Magnitude or intensity?

Although the Richter and moment magnitudes of an earthquake give an idea of its overall size, there are aspects of a quake that they do not describe, such as the intensity of the shaking, and how the earthquake affects people and buildings. To describe these aspects, a different scale again is used: the Modified Mercalli scale, which runs from 1 (no noticeable effect) to 12 (catastrophic, total destruction). Since the intensity of an earthquake is somewhat subjective and cannot be recorded by a machine, a quake's rating on the Mercalli scale is compiled by inspecting the damage and interviewing the survivors. Every earthquake has just one Richter or moment magnitude, but it has many different intensities, which decrease with increasing distance from the earthquake's epicentre.

RICHTER SCALE

The Richter scale measures the magnitude of an earthquake – the amount of energy released at the source as determined by seismographs. It has no upper limit.

1.0–2.0	Micro and minor earthquakes that are not felt, but are recorded. Relates to Mercalli scale 1.
3.0–3.9	Minor earthquakes that are felt by people. Relates to Mercalli scale 2–3.
4.0–4.9	Light earthquakes, with obvious effects such as rattling and breaking of dishes. Relates to Mercalli scale 4–5.
5.0–5.9	Moderate earthquakes that can greatly damage poorly built structures. Relates to Mercalli scale 6–7.
6.0–6.9	Strong. Can destroy buildings over large areas. Relates to Mercalli scale 7–9.
>7.0	Major. Causes serious damage over large areas. Relates to Mercalli scale 8 and above.

COURSE OF A QUAKE

IN MOST CASES, LARGE EARTHQUAKES GIVE NO CLUE THAT THEY ARE ABOUT TO HAPPEN. The first thing that people near the epicentre feel is a sudden large jolt or thud as though a giant with a sledgehammer had struck the ground from below. This effect is due to the arrival of the first, fastest-moving waves from the quake's focus, called the primary or P waves. Because these are compressional waves, they cause jolting rather than side-to-side shaking. For smaller or more distant quakes, the first P waves can produce just a gentle bump.

Shake, rattle and roll

Around the epicentre of a large quake, the initial jolt is quickly followed by violent shaking caused by arrival of the quake's secondary or S waves and the surface waves that follow after these. The pattern of this shaking can be complex, involving rolling or undulating movements, because the secondary waves tend to move the ground from side to side, while the surface waves move it up and down. In most quakes the shaking lasts for less than a minute, but it can go on for several minutes.

People who are indoors when a quake strikes will typically witness furniture being moved around, and the contents of shelves falling to the floor or being thrown across the room. Ceilings collapse, windows shatter and large cracks appear in walls. Someone in the midst of all this chaos may find it difficult to stand up, let alone reach a door and escape from the building.

Many people report hearing unusual noises at the start of an earthquake – anything from a loud bang or explosion to a roar or rumble. Experts think that most of these sounds result from buildings vibrating and their contents moving around, although this cannot account for the noises heard by people during earthquakes in the countryside. Another explanation is that the lower-pitched sounds heard at the beginning of the quake are caused by the quake's P waves travelling from the ground into the air, where they effectively become airborne soundwaves.

BUILDING FAILURE A line of cars was crushed when the supports for an underground car park collapsed during an earthquake in Los Angeles in 1995.

FREEWAY DEVASTATION A section of Interstate 880 in Oakland, California, wrecked during a major earthquake in October 1989 (right).

The shaking phase of an earthquake causes significant vertical and horizontal movements of the land surface. The ground may seem to undulate, and cracks may appear in it. Contrary to popular belief, these cracks hardly ever widen into gaping chasms that swallow up buildings and people. The cracks remain cracks, but the ground on either side of the crack may move in different directions – either side to side, up and down, or in a complex corkscrew motion.

Soil liquefaction

When severely shaken by earthquake waves, some soils undergo a process called liquefaction. This greatly reduces the strength and stiffness of the soil, diminishing its ability to bear loads. Liquefaction is most likely to occur in ground that is saturated with water, or at least has a high water content. Under normal conditions the water exerts a pressure on the soil particles, which influences how tightly the particles themselves are packed together. Before an earthquake, the water pressure is relatively low and the soil is stable. However, the shaking during a quake can increase the water pressure to the point where the soil particles start moving around – the soil has become liquefied.

Soil in this liquefied state begins to behave like a fluid, and any building sitting on it will start to sink into the ground. Some buildings collapse completely; others may still be left standing after the earthquake, but leaning at

FIRE STORM *Within minutes of the 1995 Kobe earthquake, 300 fires had broken out (right). Sparks from severed electrical cables ignited leaking gas from ruptured pipes.*

EMERGENCY RESPONSE *A fire crew attempts to rescue survivors from a collapsed, burning building in Taipei in 1999 (below). The epicentre of the earthquake was some 150km south of the city, in a small town called Chi-Chi.*

crazy angles. Soil liquefaction can also cause buried objects, such as pipelines and even coffins, to rise to the surface.

Building collapse

The chances of a structure collapsing depend on several factors, including the nature of the ground supporting the foundations of the building, the materials used and the buildings' design. Structures built on top of solid bedrock generally move as a unit with the ground and suffer the least damage during an earthquake. Structures on poorly consolidated material or water-saturated ground are much more vulnerable to collapse or subsidence, partly because such material is subject to longer shaking, but also because the side to side movement of S waves become amplified in these types of ground. Non-reinforced brick and concrete structures have no flexibility and tend to collapse. Mud-walled buildings are even weaker and tend to disintegrate entirely. In contrast, buildings with frames of either resilient wood or well-knit steel and reinforced concrete are much more likely to withstand the shaking and survive.

As well as destroying buildings, the shaking associated with an earthquake is liable to trigger landslides in mountainous regions or in coastal areas overlooked by cliffs, although this seldom occurs farther than 40–50 km from the quake's epicentre. In mountains with large glaciers, disintegration of the ice and underlying earth and rock following a quake can produce torrents of mudflows; earthquakes can also trigger snow avalanches. These mass movements can themselves sometimes cause devastating disasters and large numbers of deaths.

Outbreaks of fire

Fires often follow earthquakes because ground movement breaks underground gas pipes. Sparks from electrical cables or other electrical equipment, also damaged by the quake, then ignite the escaping gas. Such fires can be particularly devastating because the destruction already caused by the quake severely hinders the attempts of fire services to reach the flames. To make matters worse, when they do reach the fires, there is often no water supply to douse them. As much as 90 per cent of the property damage in the 1906 San Francisco earthquake was the result of fires following the quake.

AFTERMATH

WHEN A LARGE EARTHQUAKE HITS A CITY, ONE OF THE WORST EFFECTS IS THE DAMAGE TO INFRASTRUCTURE. The earthquake damages supply lines of gas, water and electricity; highways collapse, railway lines become twisted and deformed, while roads are blocked with debris from collapsed or damaged buildings. All of this greatly hinders rescue efforts.

The aftermath of a large quake is usually chaotic. One survivor of the 1906 San Francisco earthquake said it was 'bedlam, pandemonium, and hell rolled into one'. Dust and smoke fill the air, scores of voices call out for help. Glass and debris of all shapes and sizes litter the ground. The physical landscape is distorted – a once-familiar view may be unrecognisable. Some areas of ground could have been raised – perhaps by up to

SEARCHING IN HOPE A sniffer dog searches for signs of survivors beneath the rubble after a quake in Mexico City.

several metres – while others have sunk down from previous positions. And some areas will show no sign at all of the intense disruption they have just been through.

And it isn't over...

Once the main release of energy in an earthquake has occurred, a series of smaller earthquakes, called aftershocks, usually follow. These are extremely dangerous as they can cause the total collapse of buildings that were only partly damaged in the main quake. Aftershocks result from continuing adjustments in the rock fault that ruptured to produce the main shock. Sometimes, after what was thought to be the main shock, an even bigger earthquake occurs. This is then considered to be the main shock, and the earlier large quake is called a foreshock.

An earthquake large enough to cause damage is usually followed by several aftershocks within the first hour. After that, the rate of aftershocks slowly decreases. The second day has about half the number of aftershocks; the third day has about a third, and so on. Large aftershocks can occur months or even years after the main quake. Aftershocks make the challenge even more difficult for those trying to clear up a devastated city.

KOBE
QUAKE

THE COSTLIEST NATURAL DISASTER

EVER TO BEFALL A SINGLE COUNTRY HIT JAPAN IN 1995. In the early hours of January 17, many people were asleep when a section of rock at the northern end of Awaji Island fractured 25 km beneath the sea. The earthquake that ensued caused more than 6400 deaths and 26 000 injuries, most of them in Kobe, 20 km away on the Japanese island of Honshu. During the quake, the ground moved up to 50 cm horizontally and up to 1 m vertically. In the centre of Kobe, pavements were churned up and buildings left tilted – if they did not collapse entirely. In the countryside, large cracks appeared in the ground and rice fields were thrown far out of level. One spectacular casualty was the Hanshin Expressway (below), an elevated highway linking Kobe to Osaka. A 630 m section toppled over onto its side, throwing 50 cars onto the streets below. Kobe faced years of reconstruction to overcome the quake's impact, though most utility services were working by July 1995. By January 1999, 134 000 new housing units had been built, but some of the 300 000 people made homeless by the disaster were still living in temporary accommodation.

VITAL STATISTICS

DURATION: 20 seconds
RICHTER MAGNITUDE: 7.2
FATALITIES: 6430
BUILDINGS DESTROYED: more than 100 000
ECONOMIC COST: 10 trillion yen (more than $100 billion)

STORIES OF TERRIBLE EARTHQUAKES APPEAR IN THE EARLIEST WRITTEN RECORDS. These historical documents provide clues to the intensity and magnitude of ancient quakes, though the precise details have been lost. It is known, for example, that a large quake shook China in 1177 BC, but the actual magnitude of the quake remains unknown. Other early quakes include one in 1100 BC, which is said to have destroyed the ancient city of Troy. Around 1000 BC, a major earthquake struck in the Middle East at a place called Har Megiddo. Curiously this is precisely the site, according to the biblical Book of Revelation, where a climactic battle will occur at the end of the world – Armageddon. Of the thousands of major earthquakes that have occurred since then, a number have acquired particular fame or notoriety.

Moving earth

In 373 BC, a large earthquake destroyed the ancient Greek city of Helike, on the south-western shore of the Gulf of Corinth. The quake was closely followed by a tsunami, and by the morning the whole of Helike, and a substantial area of land separating it from the sea, had sunk down and was underwater. The city's 5000 inhabitants are presumed to have drowned. According to the Greek historian Callisthenes, some 'immense columns of fire' had

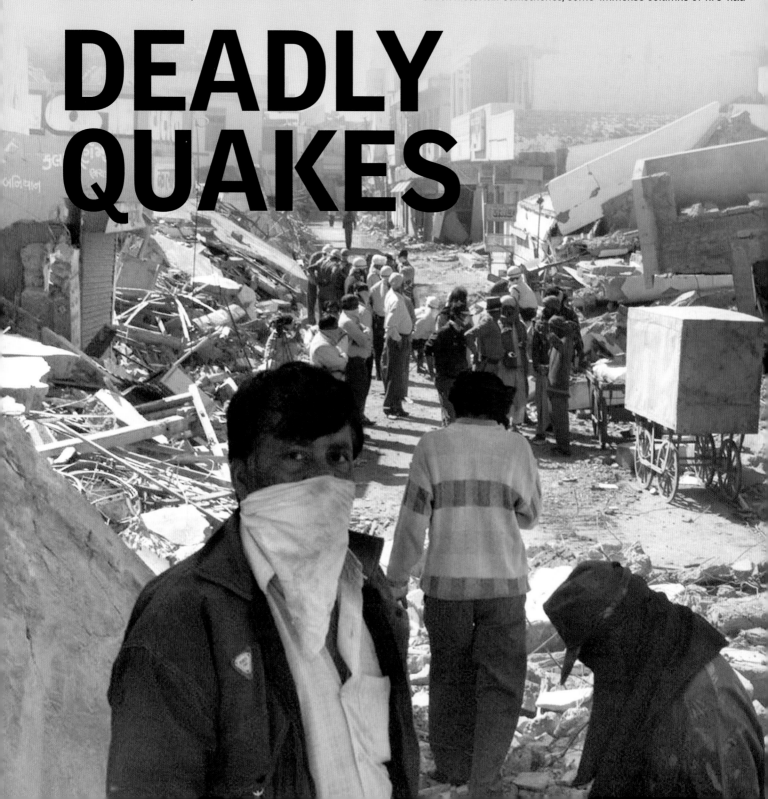

DEADLY QUAKES

THE TEN DEADLIEST QUAKES IN HISTORY

Earthquakes have caused widespread death and destruction throughout history. The worst fatalities occur when the epicentre lies close to a heavily populated or built-up area. Many of the deaths are caused by phenomena associated with earthquakes rather than the quake itself, such as avalanches, landslides and tsunamis. In recent years the Boxing Day tsunami of 2004 – generated by an earthquake in the Indian Ocean – caused widespread devastation across 13 countries in southern Asia.

PLACE	DATE	FACTS
Shaanxi, China	January 23, 1556	Fatalities: 830 000. Richter magnitude: 8.0–8.3 (estimated). Many people in the region lived in caves dug out of loess cliffs, which collapsed.
Tangshan, China	July 28, 1976	Fatalities: 243 000 officially, other estimates say as many as 750 000. Richter magnitude: 7.8. In Tangshan, 93 per cent of homes were destroyed.
Off northern Sumatra, Indian Ocean	December 26, 2004	Fatalities: 230 000. Richter magnitude: 9.3, the second-strongest ever recorded, triggering a deadly tsunami that swept across the Indian Ocean.
Aleppo, Syria	August 9, 1138	Fatalities: 230 000 – the figure is now thought to include deaths from two other quakes in the Middle East during 1137–39. Richter magnitude: unknown.
Damghan, Iran	December 22, 856	Fatalities: 200 000. Richter magnitude: unknown.
Ningxia-Gansu, China	December 16, 1920	Fatalities: 200 000. Richter magnitude: 8.6 (estimated).
Tsinghai, China	May 22, 1927	Fatalities: 200 000. Richter magnitude: 7.9 (estimated).
Ardabil, Iran	March 23, 893	Fatalities: 150 000. Richter magnitude: unknown.
Kanto, Japan	September 1, 1923	Fatalities: 143 000. Richter magnitude: 7.9–8.4 (estimated). Many of the deaths were due to firestorms in Tokyo and Yokohama, and a 10 m high tsunami.
Ashgabat, Turkmenistan	October 6, 1948	Fatalities: 110 000. Richter magnitude: 7.3 (estimated).

appeared in the area shortly before the disaster and many animals fled south into the mountains. The submerged city's remains were rediscovered in 2001. Some experts believe that Helike could have inspired the legend of the lost city of Atlantis.

The Shaanxi earthquake of 1556, which affected a large area of central and eastern China, was the most deadly in history, killing 830 000 people. At the time, a high proportion of people in the region lived in caves dug out of loess cliffs (a type of loosely formed crumbly soil formed from windblown silt). During the quake, many of these caves collapsed, accounting for the huge loss of life. The deformation of the land caused by the earthquake is still visible in parts of Shaanxi province today.

Stricken cities

Along with a quake in Messina, Sicily, in 1908, the Lisbon earthquake of 1755 is ranked as one of the two deadliest in European history. It struck on the morning of November 1, with shaking that lasted for several minutes. Following the tremor,

TOWN DESTROYED In 2001 the main street of Bhachau, in the state of Gujarat, lay in ruins following a Richter scale 7.9 quake – India's second most powerful quake on record.

survivors watched in fascination as the sea receded from the city's harbours and nearby coastline, revealing the remains of ancient shipwrecks. But 40 minutes later, a massive tsunami struck and engulfed a large part of the city: the quake's epicentre is reckoned to have been in the Atlantic some 280 km to the south-west of Lisbon.

In the areas of the city not struck by the tsunami, fires broke out and raged for five days. Lisbon was almost completely destroyed, and between 60 000 and 100 000 people perished. Geologists have estimated that the quake – caused by the African Plate being subducted under the Eurasian Plate – had a Richter magnitude of 8.7, making it one of the most powerful earthquakes in history.

A little more than 250 years after the Lisbon catastrophe, North America had its deadliest earthquake on record. Like others in San Francisco before and since, the quake of 1906 was caused by a rupture along the San Andreas Fault that runs through western and southern California. Its Richter magnitude has been estimated at 7.7–8.2. Hundreds of trapped people died when tenement buildings collapsed as the ground liquefied beneath them. As with Lisbon, a major factor in the high death toll, estimated to have been at least 3000, was the outbreak of fires shortly after the quake. These burned for five days.

The deadliest earthquake of the 20th century occurred in northern China in 1976. It is notable both for its huge death toll, and for the warning signs that preceded it. These included unusual lights and animal behaviour, such as dogs continuously barking and chickens acting wildly. The Chinese Academy of Sciences had warned of an increased risk of a quake two years previously on the basis of abnormal crustal deformation, but scientists could not say when or where the quake would occur. It struck suddenly, with its epicentre close to the major city of Tangshan. The level of destruction was extreme – 93 per cent of homes and almost 80 per cent of industrial buildings were destroyed or badly damaged.

In 1985, a quake measuring 8.1 on the Richter scale hit Mexico City. It was caused by a slippage of the Cocos Plate beneath the North American Plate, some 350 km off the west coast of Mexico. The tremor lasted for an almost unprecedented 3 to 4 minutes and was felt over a vast area. The number of fatalities in the quake is disputed. According to the Mexican government it was 9000, but many residents of Mexico City estimate that the true number exceeded 60 000. The worst of the damage occurred in a part of the city built on an ancient lakebed, where the soil liquefied and caused dramatic subsidence.

On May 21, 2003, a severe earthquake hit a densely populated area of northern Algeria in the evening, just as people had settled down at home. The main quake, which was felt as far as the Spanish coast, had a magnitude of 6.8 and wrought

KASHMIR

BAM

DESTROYED VILLAGE The city of Balakot (left) was close to the epicentre of the Kashmir quake in 2005 and suffered the worst damage. Poorly constructed concrete buildings collapsed as the ground shook.

destruction in the capital, Algiers, and several cities to its east. Entire apartment blocks were reduced to rubble and other buildings were badly damaged. Over 2200 people were killed and another 10 000 injured, while 150 000 were made homeless.

Poor housing

An earthquake in Bam, Iran, in 2003 killed 26 271 people – about 30 per cent of Bam's population – and injured around 30 000. At 6.6, the Richter magnitude of this quake was relatively low to cause such destruction. The high death toll was due to the disintegration of the mud-brick structures in which a large proportion of people in Bam lived. People were buried in suffocating piles of earth, rather than trapped in voids and air pockets as typically occurs when concrete buildings collapse.

In 2005, Kashmir was hit by an earthquake measuring 7.6 on the Richter scale. The quake affected a highly mountainous region of the Indian subcontinent that is the subject of a territorial dispute between India and Pakistan. The focus of the quake was just 26 km below the land surface in a spot where the Indian Plate is colliding with the Eurasian Plate. Most of the damage was sustained within the Pakistan-administered part of Kashmir. More than 73 000 people died there, a high proportion of the fatalities being attributed to the collapse of buildings constructed from non-reinforced concrete. If reinforced concrete had been used, the death toll would have been much lower. A particular feature of this quake was the large number of landslides triggered by the earthquake, which blocked roads into the region, badly hindering relief efforts.

ALGERIA

DIGGING FOR SURVIVORS At Reghaia in northern Algeria (left), rescuers search the rubble of destroyed buildings following a powerful quake in 2003.

RESCUE MISSION In the immediate aftermath of the Mexico City quake of 1985, thousands of residents join in efforts to free those trapped under the rubble. Unofficial estimates indicate that as many as 60 000 may have died.

LOST CITADEL The 6.6 Richter magnitude quake in Bam in 2003 largely destroyed the 2500-year-old citadel, a World Heritage Site (above). The structure's unfired clay bricks crumbled in the onslaught.

MEXICO CITY

THE FOCUS OF MANY EARTHQUAKES OCCURS BENEATH THE SEA FLOOR. Most of these submarine earthquakes are the result of massive ruptures along the fault planes that separate plates at ocean-ocean and ocean-continent convergent boundaries. Nine of the ten strongest earthquakes between 1905 and 2005 happened beneath the sea floor, seven of them occurring around the Pacific Ring of Fire. These megathrust earthquakes, as they are known, are among the world's largest.

Powerful waves

The rupture that causes a megathrust earthquake results in a large block of crust at the edge of one plate driving down beneath the edge of its neighbouring plate. At the same time, the edge of the overriding plate is suddenly thrust upwards by several metres. When this occurs over a large section of the sea floor, as happens with most submarine megathrust quakes, the sudden movement displaces the overlying seawater and this generates a tsunami – a series of fast-moving, long-wavelength waves that can travel vast distances across an ocean. Although these waves unleash colossal destruction on reaching land,

SUBMARINE QUAKES

they are barely visible on the ocean surface out at sea. The term 'tsunami' actually means 'harbour wave' and was coined by Japanese fishermen who, unaware of any unusual waves while out at sea, returned to find their harbours devastated.

The Indian Ocean earthquake

A classic example of a tsunami-generating submarine quake was the tremor that caused the Indian Ocean tsunami of December 26, 2004. With a magnitude of 9.3, this quake was so large it shook the entire planet, which vibrated back and forth by over a centimetre. The earthquake resulted from a sudden rupture along a fault line where the Indian Plate is being subducted beneath the small Burma Plate. The rupture caused a slippage of about 15 m between the plates over a total length of 1200 km. The raising of the seabed displaced an estimated 30 km³ of seawater, triggering the tsunami.

Following the quake, there were several aftershocks, including one in March 2005 that in itself was the seventh-largest earthquake recorded over the past 100 years. The total energy released by the Indian Ocean earthquake has been estimated at about 10^{18} joules

(a billion billion joules), or 250 megatons – about five times larger than the biggest nuclear bomb. This makes it one of the two largest natural releases of explosive energy ever recorded, exceeded only by an earthquake that occurred off Chile in 1960.

Great Chilean earthquake

Being so recent, the 2004 Indian Ocean submarine quake and tsunami is the best remembered event of its kind. Similar events have occurred in the recent past, but are less well remembered because the destruction was not so huge and news reporting was less intense. In May 1960, for example, the largest earthquake ever recorded occurred in the south-eastern Pacific, with its epicentre 10 km off the coast of Chile. Measuring 9.5 on the Richter scale, this was a megathrust earthquake. It produced a tsunami that crossed the entire Pacific Ocean, reaching the Aleutian Islands, Japan and the Philippines, where waves up to 11 m high were recorded. The Hawaiian Islands suffered major destruction, and the coast of Chile itself was battered by 25 m high waves. The total death toll was estimated at 6000.

UNSTOPPABLE FORCE A gigantic wall of water smashes into a seawall near Penang, Malaysia, after the Indian Ocean quake of 2004.

PREDICTION AND CONTROL

EARTHQUAKE LIGHTS *These lights were photographed at night during a series of quakes that struck Japan in 1966. Similar lights have been reported before or during other quakes. They may be caused by electrically charged gas that is emitted by rock masses under great pressure in earthquake zones.*

QUAKE-PROOF UTILITIES *This earthquake-proofed tunnel, carrying water, telephone and electricity lines, has been constructed 40 m beneath the streets of Tokyo.*

EARTHQUAKE PREDICTION IS DIFFICULT. THOUGH WE CAN SAY WITH SOME CERTAINTY WHERE EARTHQUAKES ARE LIKELY TO STRIKE, WE CANNOT SAY EXACTLY WHEN. The Holy Grail of seismologists is a method for short-term prediction that would pinpoint a city about to be hit by an earthquake in a few days' time. The city could then be evacuated, saving thousands of lives, and other precautions could be taken. Unfortunately, although at least one successful prediction of this type has been made in the past (in China), earthquake prediction has generally not yet reached this level of precision. Ideally, a prediction system must be not just accurate, but consistently accurate and reliable. A system that has the occasional success but also regularly predicts earthquakes that do not happen, or fails to predict earthquakes that do happen, is of little value.

Chinese earthquake prediction

The story of earthquake prediction in China over the past 30 years or so provides a good illustration of some of the problems involved. In February 1975, an earthquake of magnitude of 7.3 struck the densely populated town of Haicheng in north-eastern China. Damage to the city was extensive, but relatively few lives were lost because Chinese scientists had predicted the quake a few days beforehand, based on a combination of unusual animal behaviour and geophysical measurements. The scientists predicted four other sizeable earthquakes during 1975–76.

Then, in July 1976, they failed to provide a firm prediction of the Tangshan earthquake (see page 52). Although warning signs were noticed, they were scattered over too large an area to pinpoint the quake's exact location in advance. The failure to predict this large quake led experts to question whether the previous predictions might

DISASTER DRILL Children in Tokyo take part in a disaster drill, considered essential given the risk of quakes striking the city.

not just have been lucky coincidences. Since the 1970s, Chinese earthquake prediction has continued to have mixed results.

Looking for signs

One of the prediction methods used over the years by Chinese scientists and others involves watching the behaviour of animals. The imminent arrival of a large earthquake has been linked to snakes coming out of hibernation in mid-winter, dogs barking continuously, hens laying fewer eggs and pigs biting each other. Bees have been reported evacuating their hives, deep-sea fish have come up to the surface of the oceans and so on. The theory behind animal prediction is that animals are more sensitive than humans to changes inside the Earth. They may, for example, be picking up ultrasonic waves from microearthquakes as rock begins to fracture along a fault.

Most earthquake scientists are sceptical about the value of monitoring animals. Instead, they focus their efforts on measuring various geophysical phenomena. One of these is the level of water in wells. Research in China and Japan has found that the level of water in deep wells in an earthquake zone drops in the years prior to a large quake, then rises sharply again shortly before a shock, probably due to increased pressure in the rocks reducing the volume of space in the tiny rock pores that hold water.

Other signs monitored by scientists include ground uplift and tilting due to the swelling of rocks caused by strain building up in the fault; the emission of radon gas as rocks deform; and phenomena such as unusual radio waves, which can occur just prior to some major earthquakes. None of the various types of precursor event has so far proved consistently useful for predicting quakes. This may be because earthquakes in different regions behave differently.

Earthquake control

For several decades, it has been known that the injection of high-pressure fluids deep into the ground in earthquake zones can lubricate faults, triggering several small earthquakes long before the strain energy has built up to cause a large one. But the possibility of using this as earthquake control needs more study. Part of the problem is the amount of energy involved in a large earthquake. For every increase in earthquake magnitude, there is a 30-fold increase in the amount of explosive energy released. So if you are triggering acceptably small quakes of magnitude 4, you would need to generate more than 800 000 of them to release the same energy as a magnitude 8 earthquake.

BUILDING PROTECTION

CERTAIN PARTS OF THE WORLD ARE PRONE TO EARTHQUAKES AND SO ARE LIKELY TO SUFFER MORE IN THE FUTURE. Tokyo and San Francisco, for example, can be reasonably certain that a large earthquake will occur in their vicinity some time in the next 100 years. Fortunately for these cities, they belong to two of the world's wealthiest nations and have the means to finance adequate precautions, which include incorporating features into new buildings to make them earthquake-proof, improving the quake-resistance of existing buildings and developing adequate evacuation plans. But many of the world's other large earthquake-prone cities – including Mexico City, Manila (Philippines), San Salvador (El Salvador) and Tashkent (Uzbekistan) – are in poorer nations, which are much less well-placed to fund this level of protection.

Protection for all

One solution is to develop low-cost, earthquake-proof housing solutions that can be used in earthquake zones worldwide. A recent prototype that uses a combination of steel, concrete and bamboo as the main building materials has been successfully tested. The erected houses were set on a layer of discarded automobile tyres that acted as a low-cost shock absorber/damper

mechanism. The buildings were found to withstand a level of shaking equivalent to an earthquake of Richter magnitude 10.

A number of design features can be incorporated into modern buildings in earthquake zones to reduce the chances of them being damaged or collapsing during a quake. They include the use of steel-reinforced concrete; cross-braces, which resist stress better than rectangular frames; and base isolators, which allow buildings to move independently of the ground during a quake. It is also important to ensure that the external parts of structures do not disintegrate, with the risk of causing serious injury in the street below. Façades are securely fastened onto the buildings' frames, and windows are made from specially strengthened, shatterproof glass.

Absorbing the shocks

Skyscrapers in earthquake zones have to be anchored particularly deeply and securely into the ground and need a reinforced framework with stronger joints than an ordinary skyscraper. Embedded within the structure are numerous sophisticated shock-absorbing devices called dampers. These use any of various systems of large springs, fluid-filled pistons and pendulums to absorb or dissipate energy during an earthquake and thus reduce swaying and vibration.

Workplaces, homes and schools in earthquake zones must have all their heavy furniture and appliances securely fastened down to prevent them from toppling when the building shakes. Water and gas lines must be specially reinforced with flexible joints to prevent breakage.

The siting of buildings is as important as the design. Geological mapping of earthquake zones can identify areas where the ground is most likely to liquefy during an earthquake, where landslides may happen and where substantial movement is likely to occur around faults. These areas are then allocated to uses that are less sensitive to seismic activity, such as agriculture, while safer, more stable areas are assigned for building development.

ANCIENT DESIGN The Yasaka Pagoda in Kyoto, Japan, has withstood centuries of earthquakes thanks to structural features such as a central pillar. Engineers are now adapting these features for modern use.

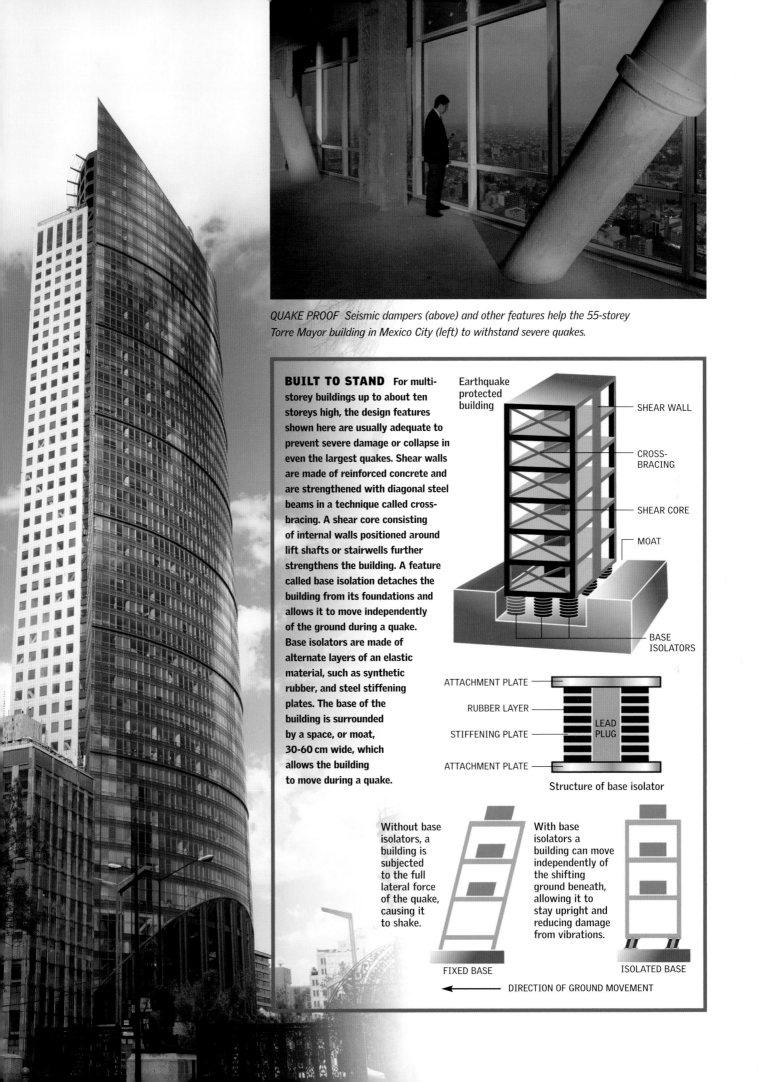

QUAKE PROOF Seismic dampers (above) and other features help the 55-storey Torre Mayor building in Mexico City (left) to withstand severe quakes.

BUILT TO STAND For multi-storey buildings up to about ten storeys high, the design features shown here are usually adequate to prevent severe damage or collapse in even the largest quakes. Shear walls are made of reinforced concrete and are strengthened with diagonal steel beams in a technique called cross-bracing. A shear core consisting of internal walls positioned around lift shafts or stairwells further strengthens the building. A feature called base isolation detaches the building from its foundations and allows it to move independently of the ground during a quake. Base isolators are made of alternate layers of an elastic material, such as synthetic rubber, and steel stiffening plates. The base of the building is surrounded by a space, or moat, 30-60 cm wide, which allows the building to move during a quake.

Earthquake protected building

SHEAR WALL

CROSS-BRACING

SHEAR CORE

MOAT

BASE ISOLATORS

ATTACHMENT PLATE

RUBBER LAYER

STIFFENING PLATE

LEAD PLUG

ATTACHMENT PLATE

Structure of base isolator

Without base isolators, a building is subjected to the full lateral force of the quake, causing it to shake.

With base isolators a building can move independently of the shifting ground beneath, allowing it to stay upright and reducing damage from vibrations.

FIXED BASE

ISOLATED BASE

DIRECTION OF GROUND MOVEMENT

WHEN EARTH ERUPTS

R

3

VOLCANIC ERUPTIONS ARE SOME OF THE EARTH'S MOST DRAMATIC SPECTACLES, PROOF THAT OUR PLANET IS A DYNAMIC AND EVER-CHANGING BODY. During a major eruption, a volcano such as Mount Etna (seen here in 2002) can alter the physical landscape over thousands of square kilometres, decimate cities and even affect world climate. Over the past four centuries, volcanic activity has killed more than 300 000 people worldwide, mainly as a result of devastating flows of hot gases and ash, mudflows and tsunamis. With an increasing proportion of the world's human population living in volcanic areas, an estimated 500 million people are now at an appreciable risk from such disasters. That poses a formidable challenge for scientists aiming to provide timely and reliable warnings of where and when major eruptions will occur.

WHAT IS A VOLCANO?

VOLCANOES ARE PLACES WHERE RED-HOT MAGMA COMES TO THE SURFACE. But why do volcanoes erupt? And why does magma spew out gently from one volcano, while from another it bursts out violently in a torrent of ash, gas and lava bombs? The widest definition of a volcano is any opening in the Earth's crust through which hot magma – produced by the melting of rocks in the Earth's upper mantle and lower crust – can escape to the surface. Volcanologists prefer to restrict the term to structures in

EQUATORIAL VOLCANO
A cloud of steam and ash rises from Tungurahua, a 5000 m high volcano, located just south of the equator in Ecuador.

which magma and the gases it contains surge up from a magma chamber to the surface via a vertical channel, or vent. The chamber lies at least 5 km deep – sometimes as deep as 50 km or more.

Volcanoes build up from the accumulation of material from their own eruptions. Magma is exceedingly hot, with a temperature of anything between 700°C and 1200°C. As the magma erupts from the vent and then cools, it leaves a solid deposit of ash, cinders or lava that gradually grows larger. The most familiar volcanic form is a steep-sided conical mountain, which can be thousands of metres high. But volcanoes also take other forms – anything from much smaller cones to extensive, flat areas of lava or large, water-filled depressions in the landscape.

In addition to the central vent common to all volcanoes, many also have narrow channels that branch off from the main vent. These are called side vents, or branch pipes. Magma that comes surging up these conduits can create mini-volcanoes on the flanks of the main volcano. Secondary or parasitic cones can sometimes grow extremely large, but they are not considered as volcanoes in their own right.

At the apex of most volcanoes is a bowl-shaped depression, called a crater, which contains the mouth of the vent. The majority of craters are created when large explosions of material from the vent blow out the apex of the cone. Some volcanoes have particularly large craters, which have formed by a more gradual process of collapse at the summit. In a volcano that has been quiet for a while, the mouth of the vent may be completely filled in with a mass of cooled and hardened lava, called a volcanic plug. In such cases, the crater will often be filled with water, producing a crater lake.

What triggers an eruption?

Many factors combine to determine exactly when an eruption will be triggered and what sort of eruption it will be. They include the amount of magma in a volcano, the magma's chemical composition, the percentage of water and dissolved gases it contains and the pressure within the magma chamber. These factors vary from one volcano to another and determine why some volcanoes erupt frequently and fairly mildly, while others erupt infrequently but explosively.

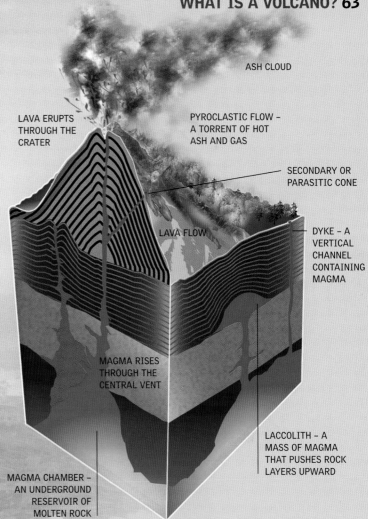

ASH CLOUD

LAVA ERUPTS THROUGH THE CRATER

PYROCLASTIC FLOW – A TORRENT OF HOT ASH AND GAS

SECONDARY OR PARASITIC CONE

LAVA FLOW

DYKE – A VERTICAL CHANNEL CONTAINING MAGMA

MAGMA RISES THROUGH THE CENTRAL VENT

LACCOLITH – A MASS OF MAGMA THAT PUSHES ROCK LAYERS UPWARD

MAGMA CHAMBER – AN UNDERGROUND RESERVOIR OF MOLTEN ROCK

STRUCTURE OF A VOLCANO All volcanoes contain at least one vent – a central channel that carries magma upwards from the magma chamber. Some also contain side vents. At the mouth of the vent, there is usually a crater from which different types of material may spew out. The wind carries away fine ash. Larger fragments fall back around the vent – accumulations of these fragments gradually move down the slopes of the volcano. Lava and pyroclastic flows stream down the volcano's flanks.

In many cases, the specific trigger for an eruption is the sudden welling up of new magma into an already filled magma chamber. This forces some of the existing magma upwards. As the magma rises and its pressure decreases, the dissolved water and gases within it start to form bubbles, which begin to expand fast. When the volume of bubbles within the magma reaches about 75 per cent, the rock disintegrates into a mixture of partially molten and solid fragments, which are spewed explosively out of the volcano's vent.

In some volcanoes, a solid plug of lava that has formed within the upper part of the vent prevents an eruption from happening for a long period of time. Pressure gradually builds up in the magma chamber below – sometimes causing the sides of the volcano to bulge outwards – until the lava plug is literally blown out, much like a cork popping from a champagne bottle. The result is a particularly violent eruption.

IN SEARCH OF VOLCANOES

ACTIVE VOLCANOES ARE FOUND IN REGIONS WHERE MAGMA FORMS IN LARGE QUANTITIES BENEATH THE EARTH'S CRUST. Such regions occur at divergent plate boundaries (see page 22), notably mid-ocean ridges and continental rift zones; at convergent boundaries (see page 27); and at hotspots where warm mantle plumes rise up under areas of oceanic crust.

Although most volcanoes are easily spotted as cone-shaped hills and mountains rising above the landscape, the effects of rainfall, wind and water erosion, glaciation and colonisation by plants have made some far less easy to discern. In some parts of the world, extremely dangerous volcanoes lie hidden underneath features such as glaciers, large tranquil lakes or dense vegetation.

Active, dormant or extinct?

A volcano is known as 'historically active' if it has erupted at least once in recorded history. If it has erupted at least once in the past 10 000 years (the Holocene period of Earth's history), it is classed as 'Holocene active'. The distinction between the two is significant, since by the first definition there are about 550 active volcanoes, and by the second definition about 1300–1500.

An extinct volcano is one that has not erupted in the past 10 000 years and volcanologists are certain will never erupt again. That leaves 'dormant' volcanoes, which can generally be defined as active volcanoes that have not erupted for a long time (at least 100 years) but are expected to erupt again one day. An example of a dormant volcano is Mount Shasta in California. This erupts on average once every 600 years – the last time it erupted was in 1786.

ONES TO WATCH Scientists have selected 16 volcanoes, shown on this map, for special study and monitoring because of their history of violent eruptions and their proximity to population centres. Nearly all are highly active – nine of the 16 have erupted at least once since 2000.

KEY
Volcanoes
Plate boundary

MOUNT RAINIER, USA

MAUNA LOA, HAWAII

COLIMA, MEXICO

SANTA MARIA, GUATEMALA

GALERAS, COLOMBIA

GALERAS Lying close to the Colombian city of Pasto, Galeras has erupted frequently over the past 500 years. It currently contains a small dark active cone (shown here) inside a huge collapsed crater that formed following a massive explosion thousands of years ago.

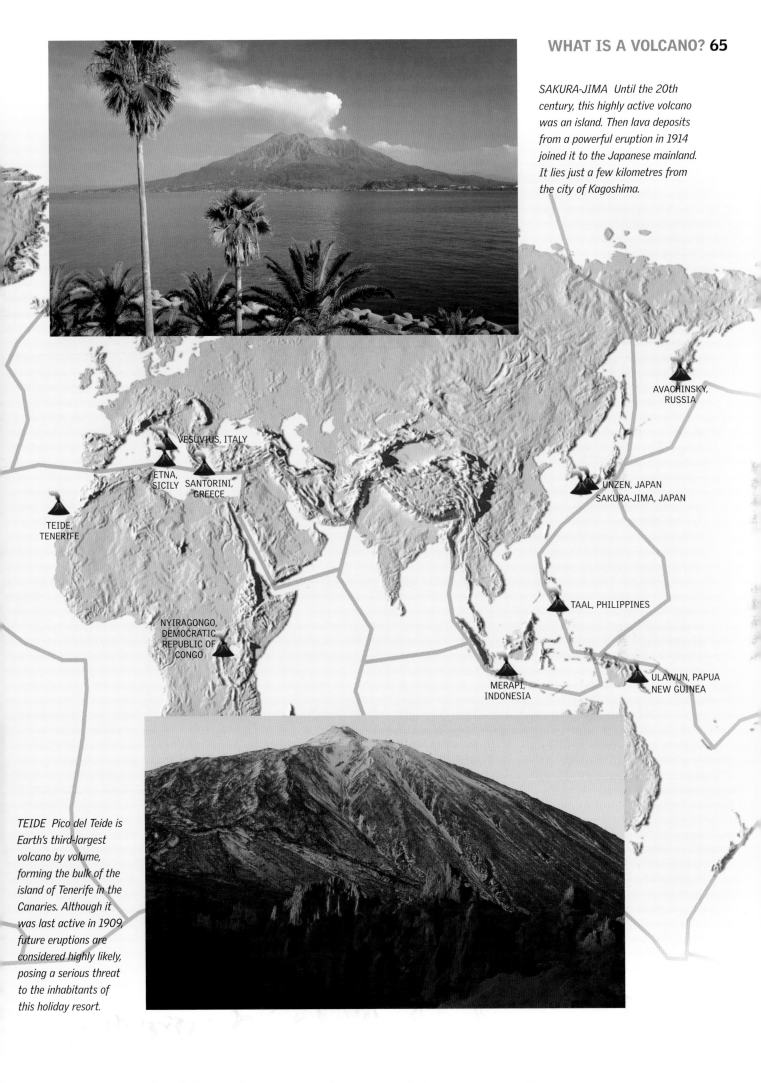

SAKURA-JIMA Until the 20th century, this highly active volcano was an island. Then lava deposits from a powerful eruption in 1914 joined it to the Japanese mainland. It lies just a few kilometres from the city of Kagoshima.

AVACHINSKY, RUSSIA

VESUVIUS, ITALY

ETNA, SICILY

SANTORINI, GREECE

UNZEN, JAPAN
SAKURA-JIMA, JAPAN

TEIDE, TENERIFE

TAAL, PHILIPPINES

NYIRAGONGO, DEMOCRATIC REPUBLIC OF CONGO

MERAPI, INDONESIA

ULAWUN, PAPUA NEW GUINEA

TEIDE Pico del Teide is Earth's third-largest volcano by volume, forming the bulk of the island of Tenerife in the Canaries. Although it was last active in 1909, future eruptions are considered highly likely, posing a serious threat to the inhabitants of this holiday resort.

TYPES OF VOLCANO

EVERY VOLCANO IS UNIQUE IN ITS FORM, BEHAVIOUR AND HISTORY, VARYING FROM OTHERS IN SIZE, SHAPE, FREQUENCY OF ERUPTION AND THE TYPE OF MATERIAL IT DISGORGES. Nevertheless, volcanologists classify volcanoes into basic types, which include shield, cinder cone, composite and caldera. The type of volcano that is likely to be found in any particular part of the world depends primarily on the properties of the magma beneath the Earth's crust in that region – especially its temperature, water content and chemical composition.

Gradual build-up

Shield volcanoes are broad volcanoes built up almost entirely from extensive lava flows. Many of them develop over mantle hotspots (see page 96). The magma that rises up beneath the Earth's crust in these regions usually has a low content of water and dissolved gases, which means that the magma is less likely to erupt explosively into the air. The high temperature and chemical composition of the magma makes it especially fluid and runny. So when the lava pours out, it tends to flow for a considerable distance – up to tens of kilometres – over the surface before it cools and solidifies.

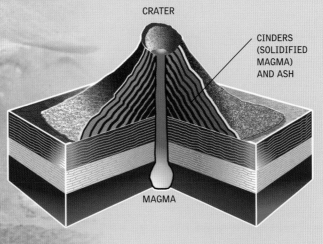

CRATER

CINDERS (SOLIDIFIED MAGMA) AND ASH

MAGMA

CINDER CONES Usually no more than 350 m high, cinder cones are small volcanoes composed largely of fragments of solidified magma (cinders). They typically have bowl-shaped craters at their summits and sometimes develop in groups, as in this line of Hawaiian cones (left).

In a shield volcano, the supply of upwelling magma is usually fairly constant, so eruptions tend to occur frequently. The lava may flow out of a central summit vent, which is often contained within a wide crater, or from a group of vents. Lava also commonly erupts from vents along fractures, called rift zones, or from parasitic cones on the flanks of the volcano.

Small cones

Cinder cones are relatively small conical volcanoes built up from blobs of congealed magma ejected from a single vent. As the gas-charged magma is blown violently into the air during an eruption, it breaks into glassy fragments that solidify and fall as cinders around the vent. Although most produce only cinders and sometimes a little ash, a few also erupt lava, which flows out through a breach in the side of the cone, not from the summit. An example of a cinder cone is Cerro Negro in Nicaragua, an impressive black cone that has been almost constantly active since 1850, growing to a height of 250 m.

GENTLE SLOPE OF BASALTIC LAVA FLOW

CRATER

MAGMA

SHIELD VOLCANO A large, broad volcano with gently sloping slides and a shape like an upturned warrior's shield, this type of volcano is built up from a series of lava flows. The example here is Erta Ale, a 50 km wide shield volcano in Ethiopia.

CRATER

ALTERNATING
LAYERS OF
SOLIDIFIED
LAVA AND ASH

MAGMA

COMPOSITE VOLCANO Built up from alternating layers of ash and solidified lava, a composite volcano (or stratovolcano) has the classic tall, steep-sided, conical volcano shape. Arenal (right), a highly active composite volcano in Costa Rica, is a typical example of the type.

Dangerous beauties

Composite volcanoes (also called stratovolcanoes) are tall, steep-sided volcanoes, composed of alternating layers of ash, lava and cinders. Rising to heights of up to 2500 m, they comprise some of the Earth's most famous and most beautiful mountains – but also many of its most explosively dangerous ones. The reason for this is that most have formed above convergent plate boundaries, where the magma tends to have a high content of water and dissolved gases as well as silica, which makes it highly viscous. The magma is often noisily erupted as ash and volcanic bombs. When lava emerges, it tends to cool and harden before travelling far – hence the steep-sided profile of these volcanoes.

Saucers in the landscape

Every few thousand years, a large composite volcano has a cataclysmic eruption that empties its magma chamber and destroys its cone. What remains is a wide crater with a rim – a saucer-shaped circular depression in the landscape – called a caldera. Calderas are often filled with water, forming what look like tranquil lakes. In many cases, no one except a geological expert would suspect that these depressions are volcanoes. Yet many of them are still volcanically active, with huge magma chambers lurking beneath them. Notable calderas include Crater Lake in Oregon, USA, which was formed by an explosion some 7500 years ago, and Lake Toba in Sumatra.

CALDERA A wide crater with a floor composed of material derived from the partial disintegration of an old composite volcano. Many calderas are filled with water, as here (left) at Crater Lake in Oregon, USA.

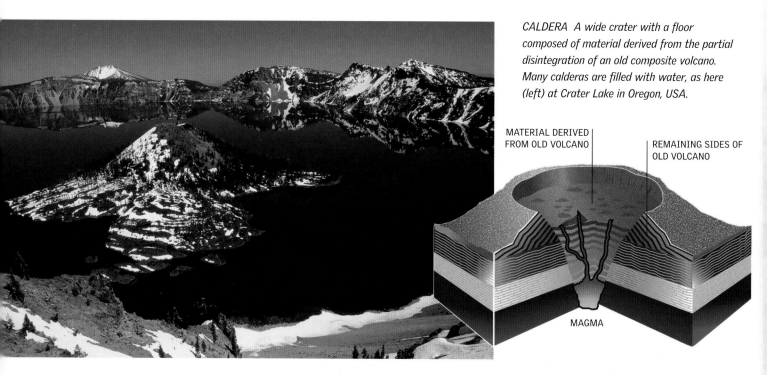

MATERIAL DERIVED
FROM OLD VOLCANO

REMAINING SIDES OF
OLD VOLCANO

MAGMA

KILAUEA

THE WORLD'S MOST ACTIVE VOLCANO,

KILAUEA HAS ERUPTED MORE THAN 40 TIMES OVER THE PAST HUNDRED YEARS. It is one of five shield volcanoes that make up the island of Hawaii. Since 1983, it has been in a state of almost continuous eruption, covering a vast area of the island in thick black lava. It is also a popular tourist attraction, known as the 'drive-by' volcano – anyone can ride by in a car while safely observing its impressive magma fountains shooting 300 m or more into the air.

Nearly all of the activity has been concentrated on Kilauea's eastern flank in a region, 20 km long, called the eastern rift zone. In 1983 gigantic ground fissures appeared that spewed out fiery lava. Within a few weeks the eruption had intensified and focused into an impressive lava fountain, producing a cone of material, technically known as a 'cinder-spatter cone', that rapidly grew to a height of more than 250 m. The flows have destroyed two towns on the flanks of the volcano, bisected a highway and created 2 km² of land, where the rivers of lava have cooled on reaching the sea.

VITAL STATISTICS

AGE: 300 000–600 000 years
HEIGHT OF SUMMIT: 1222 m
VOLUME OF LAVA ERUPTED
SINCE 1983: 2.7 km³
SURFACE AREA OF LAVA ERUPTED
SINCE 1983: More than 115 km²
RECORD HEIGHT OF LAVA
FOUNTAINS: 460 m

ERUPTION STYLES

WE USUALLY THINK OF VOLCANIC ERUPTIONS AS SUDDEN, DEVASTATING EXPLOSIONS. In fact, styles of eruption are extremely varied. Some eruptions last for hours, others for weeks, months, years or even decades. Some are violent; others are much more gentle.

The different styles of eruption that scientists have classified are sometimes identified with particular regions, such as Iceland or Hawaii, or they may be associated with specific famous volcanoes – Mount Vesuvius in southern Italy, for example, which buried the Roman cities of Herculaneum and Pompeii in AD 79. Categorising volcanoes is never straightforward because they can be notoriously capricious. Over the course of its history, a single volcano will sometimes erupt in one style and sometimes in another. Different styles can also occur during different phases of a single protracted eruption.

Icelandic and Hawaiian

The quiet outpouring of large quantities of lava from long straight fissures in the ground is a characteristic of so-called Icelandic

HAWAIIAN STYLE Spectacular lava fountains and voluminous lava rivers are typical of Hawaiian-style eruptions. This one is from a secondary cone on Nyamuragira in the Democratic Republic of Congo.

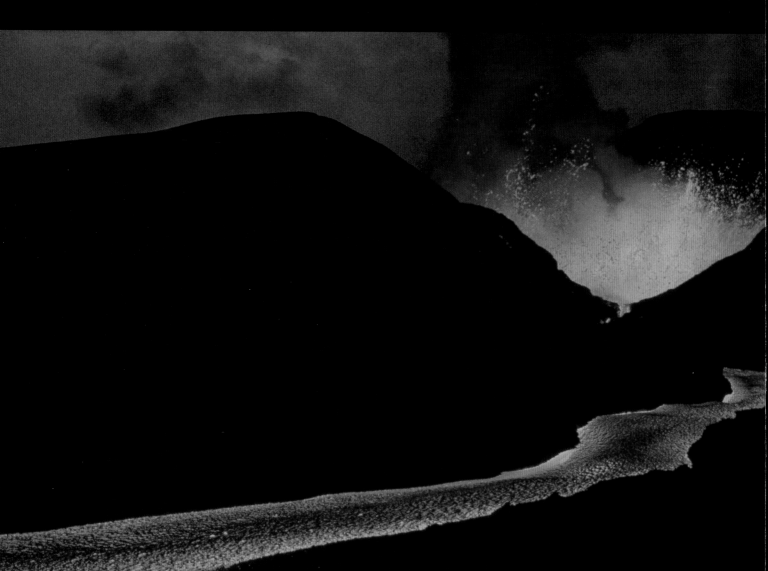

eruptions. As their name suggests, they are associated with Iceland, where in 1783 a fissure in the southern part of the country poured out more than 14 km³ of lava – the largest single emission of lava in recorded history. Over the past 50 million years, eruptions of this type have built up vast plateaus of the black volcanic rock, basalt, in various parts of the world. One of the largest is the Columbia Plateau, which covers more than 150 000 km² in the north-western USA.

A Hawaiian eruption is another of the milder, less dangerous types. It includes spectacular fountains of lava, which spew out of individual vents or from fissures in the ground and can be hundreds of metres high. Sometimes, a Hawaiian eruption involves outpourings from a lava lake within a large crater at the volcano's summit. The large Hawaiian shield volcanoes, Kilauea and Mauna Loa, most often erupt in this style.

Strombolian and Pelean

Strombolian eruptions are characterised by the emission of little bombs, or fountains, of magma from a central crater at spasmodic or rhythmic intervals. Each eruption may last for no more than a few seconds, and usually no eruption cloud develops. Strombolian eruptions that emit only aerial material build the relatively small, steep-sided types of volcanoes called cinder cones. Sometimes, Strombolian-style eruptions can be interspersed with lava flows, and this pattern of activity builds a composite volcano. They are named after Stromboli, a volcanic island in the Mediterranean off the north coast of Sicily. It is a relatively small composite volcano that has been erupting almost continuously for 2000 years.

A Pelean style of eruption is much more violent. It occurs when gas pressure suddenly forces a deep plug of cooled, solidified magma out of a volcanic vent. A massive explosion and eruption of ash occurs as gases expand violently from the vent. Pyroclastic flows – ground-hugging flows of exceedingly hot ash-laden gas (see page 80) – commonly occur with these eruptions. This eruptive style, repeated over and over again, builds up a large composite volcano. It is named after the catastrophic 1902 eruption of Mont Pelée on the Caribbean island of Martinique. When the volcano exploded, a swift and devastating pyroclastic flow buried the city of Saint-Pierre, instantly killing more than 26 000 people. Another example of a Pelean-style event was the cataclysmic eruption of Mount St Helens, Washington State, USA, in 1980.

Phreatic, Vulcanian and Vesuvian

Also known as ultravulcanian eruptions, phreatic eruptions are steam-driven explosions resulting from magma coming into contact with groundwater or seawater. The high temperature of the magma causes near-instantaneous evaporation of the water to steam, resulting in an explosion of steam, ash, rock and volcanic bombs. It is thought that the 1883 eruption of the volcanic island of Krakatau in modern Indonesia was a phreatic-style eruption. It destroyed most of the island and created the loudest sound in recorded human history. A few years later, in 1888, a phreatic eruption of the Japanese volcano Bandai claimed the lives of 461 people.

In Roman mythology, the island of Vulcano, north of Sicily, was believed to be the chimney of the workshop of Vulcan, the god of fire. The island has given its name to volcanoes as a whole and, in modern scientific terminology, to another eruption style – Vulcanian. This starts with a violent explosion caused by the removal of a plug in a vent as gases and pressure build up. Immediately following the explosion, large amounts of magma shoot out of the volcano – the eruptive columns can rise 15 km into the air. Pyroclastic flows then stream down the volcano's flanks, or ash, cinders and lava bombs fall over the surrounding countryside. Lava flows may emerge later. This eruptive style builds a large composite volcano. Volcanoes that erupt consistently in this style do so in eruptions spaced tens of years to hundreds of years apart.

Vesuvian eruptions are named after Mount Vesuvius, but the volcano in southern Italian has produced eruptions in many styles over the centuries, including Pelean, Vulcanian and Plinian. A Vesuvian eruption is an extremely violent explosion

PLINIAN STYLE The eruption of Mount Pinatubo in the Philippines in June 1991 (above) is one of the most recent examples of a Plinian-style eruption. A huge ash cloud rose 25 km into the atmosphere.

VULCANIAN STYLE An ash cloud billows from Karymsky volcano (left) in Kamchatka, Russia. Though less violent than Plinian eruptions, Vulcanian ones always start off with a very noisy explosion.

VESUVIAN STYLE Intermediate between the Vulcanian and Plinian styles is a Vesuvian eruption. Here (right), it is typified by an eruption from Vesuvius itself in March 1944 during World War II. It destroyed three villages, part of a fourth and 88 US B-25 Mitchell bombers taking part in the Allied campaign to drive the Germans out of Italy.

of gas-charged magma that releases large amounts of ash and gas. The ash and gas form a billowing cloud that typically takes a mushroom or cauliflower shape. Volcanoes that erupt consistently in this spectacular style – always large composite volcanoes – do so in eruptions hundreds or thousands of years apart.

Plinian and ultra-Plinian

The most violent and spectacularly explosive eruptions of all are also associated with Vesuvius. In Plinian-style eruptions, a steady, turbulent stream of fragmented magma and gas is released at extremely high velocity from a vent. Large volumes of material are thrown into the air forming eruption columns of ash that can reach as high as 30 km. Two examples of Plinian-style events were the famous eruption of Mount Vesuvius in AD 79 and the eruption of Mount Pinatubo in the Philippines in 1991.

Plinian eruptions are named after Pliny the Elder, the Roman author and natural philosopher, who died during the AD 79 eruption of Vesuvius, and his nephew Pliny the Younger, who observed the eruption but survived to describe it later in a letter. Eruptions that outdo even Plinian ones in their explosivity are called ultra-Plinian.

VOLCANIC EXPLOSIVITY INDEX

The volcano equivalent of the Richter scale for earthquakes is the Volcanic Explosivity Index (VEI), based on various factors, including the height of the volcanic plume and the volume of material spewed out. There is a rough equivalence between VEI level and eruption style – eruptions at levels 1 and 2 are often Strombolian, levels 3 and 4 Vulcanian, levels 5 and 6 Plinian and levels 7 and 8 ultra-Plinian.

VEI	DESCRIPTION	PLUME	MATERIAL EJECTED
0	Non-explosive	Up to 100 m	Up to 10 000 m^3
1	Gentle	100–1000 m	10 000–1 million m^3
2	Explosive	1–5 km	1–10 million m^3
3	Severe	3–15 km	10–100 million m^3
4	Cataclysmic	10-25 km	0.1–1 km^3
5	Paroxysmal	Over 25 km	1–10 km^3
6	Colossal	Over 25 km	10–100 km^3
7	Super-colossal	Over 25 km	100–1000 km^3
8	Mega-colossal	Over 25 km	Over 1000 km^3

LAVA FLOWS

DURING AN ERUPTION, LAVA OFTEN CREATES SPECTACULAR 'RIVERS OF FIRE', CALLED LAVA FLOWS, AS IT SPILLS OUT OF THE VOLCANO'S CRATER. Moving inexorably over the ground, the molten rock surrounds, buries or ignites all it encounters, including houses, roads, fields and crops. Small explosions may add to the drama as the advancing front buries vegetation, producing flammable methane gas. Lava flows like these rarely result in human deaths, because most move slowly enough for people to escape them, but death and injury can happen when onlookers approach an advancing flow too closely or their retreat is cut off by other flows.

Types of lava

When molten rock is still underground, it is called magma. After it has been erupted onto the surface, it is called lava, even though – apart from some slight cooling – it has not undergone any fundamental change. It is still red-hot molten rock, usually with a temperature of 700–1200°C. Although even the runniest lava is far more viscous (thick and gluey) than water, as long as its temperature remains high enough, it will flow over the ground under the influence of gravity, sometimes for great distances.

Volcanoes in different parts of the world produce different types of lava, which vary in their chemical composition and the temperature at which they are erupted. One group, called felsic lavas, are relatively cool with a temperature of about 700°C. They have a composition that makes them very viscous, so they form slow-moving thick

Lava fountains – jets of lava thrown hundreds of metres up in the air – can sometimes be seen at volcanic vents, and from time to time a stream of lava plunges over a cliff, producing a glowing lava cascade.

PILLOW LAVA Off Hawaii, lava sometimes emerges underwater via side-channels leading from the main vents of the island's volcanoes. Here, a diver studies lava solidifying into large rounded shapes, called 'pillows', as it contacts the seawater.

*BLOCKED HIGHWAY Flowing lava has no
respect for houses, roads, trees or most other
obstacles in its path. It burns or buries
everything it meets. Here, a flow of 'a'a lava
has engulfed a road in Hawaii.*

'A'a lava is the more viscous. Its flows are
typically 3–5 m thick, although they can be up
to 12 m, and their interiors have a temperature
of between 1000 and 1100°C. Because 'a'a
lava moves quite rapidly, wherever its surface
cools to a temperature at which it hardens, the
underlying motion tears the surface and
breaks it into jagged pieces called clinkers.
Consequently, this type of lava has a jumbled
rough surface. It moves forward somewhat
like the tread of a bulldozer. As the flow
advances, clinkers on the surface are carried
forward relative to the molten interior. The
clinkers eventually roll down the steep front of the flow and the
molten core then overrides them.

Pahoehoe lava is more fluid than 'a'a and contains more gas.
It usually has a temperature of 1100–1200°C. As the surface of a
pahoehoe flow cools, it grows a thin pliable skin, which remains
intact while the lava streams beneath it. Pahoehoe flows tend to
be less than a metre thick, with a smooth, glassy surface, which
can be billowy or undulating. Sometimes, the flow of lava inside
distorts the congealing skin, wrinkling it so that its surface
acquires a ropy texture. Pahoehoe lava typically advances as a
series of small lobes, called 'toes', that break out from the cooled
crust. Each toe is about 20–80 cm wide and 15–25 cm high. With
increasing distance from a volcanic vent, a pahoehoe flow may
change into 'a'a as it loses heat and becomes more viscous.

flows. Another group, the intermediate or andesitic lavas, are
hotter (750–900°C) and less viscous, but they can still travel
only limited distances before they cool and solidify. These lavas
are typically erupted by composite volcanoes and contribute to
the steep-sided shapes of these volcanoes. A third group, called
basaltic lavas, are hotter – typically erupted with a temperature
of 1000–1200°C – and more fluid. Because of their fluidity,
basaltic lavas can travel for long distances – tens of kilometres –
even on quite gently shelving slopes. Successive flows of basaltic
lava build up shield volcanoes.

Occasionally, the crater at the top of a volcano – typically
a shield volcano – will fill with lava but not erupt. Lava that pools
in this way is called a lava lake. These lakes do not usually last for
long; they either drain back into the magma chamber once
pressure is relieved or are erupted out of the
crater. Lava fountains – jets of lava thrown
hundreds of metres up in the air – can
sometimes be seen at volcanic vents, and from
time to time a stream of lava plunges over a
cliff, producing a glowing lava cascade.

Hawaiian-style lavas

Basaltic lavas create the most spectacular lava
flows. There are two main types of basaltic
lava: 'a'a (pronounced 'ah-ah') and pahoehoe
(pronounced 'pah-hoay-hoay'). The names
come from Hawaii, where huge streams of
both types of lava can be seen on volcanoes
such as Kilauea.

*WINDOW ON A LAVA TUBE Sometimes, lava
flows down the flanks of a volcano through
enclosed channels, called lava tubes. Here, part of
the roof of a lava tube has collapsed, creating a
window onto the river of molten rock below.*

Speed of flow

The rate at which lava flows depends on the type of lava, its temperature, the steepness of the slope and the rate at which it is being ejected at the volcanic vent. There is also a considerable difference in speed between the broad advancing front of a new lava flow and a narrow stream of lava running along an established channel.

The fastest moving lava front ever recorded reached a speed of around 100 km/h during the eruption of Mount Nyiragongo in the Democratic Republic of Congo in 1977 (see page 89). The lava produced by this volcano is particularly fluid, and on that occasion an enormous quantity was released all at once, through the sudden drainage of a large lava lake in Nyiragongo's crater.

These were exceptional circumstances. In Hawaii, fronts of 'a'a lava have been measured moving down steep slopes at up to 10 km/h, but a more common speed is about 3 km/h – most people can walk faster than this and can easily escape an advancing flow. Advancing fronts of pahoehoe lava rarely progress at more than a few metres per hour. Lava moving through an established narrow channel of solidified lava can reach much faster speeds, largely because the flow is partly

BURNING TOES A flow of pahoehoe lava advances rapidly as it pushes forward a series of lobes, called lava toes. Each new toe ignites the asphalt when it contacts the road surface.

insulated, and so cools and hardens much more slowly as it flows. These channelled flows may reach dangerous speeds of up to 40 km/h – a lot faster than people can run.

Tubes and pillows

When the upper surface of a lava flow cools, it forms a solid crust. Beneath this crust, which is an excellent thermal insulator, pahoehoe-type lava can carry on flowing as a liquid. Eventually, the flow of liquid lava may form a lava tube, a tunnel-like channel through the solid lava, which conducts molten rock for many kilometres from a volcanic vent. Tubes can be as much as 15 m wide and anywhere from a metre or two beneath the surface to 15 m. Sometimes, a space forms in the roof of a lava tube – a skylight – allowing observers to look down at the lava flowing below. If the supply of fresh lava stops, the lava tube will often empty out, leaving a length of open tunnel. The record is a 50 km tube discovered on the Hawaiian shield volcano, Mauna Loa.

Pillow lava forms when magma emerges into cold water from a submarine volcano. As the liquid lava comes into contact with the water, it solidifies fast as large rounded lumps – the 'pillows'. Similar formations can occur when pahoehoe lava enters the sea, often accompanied by sizzling plumes of steam. When an 'a'a flow reaches the sea, the result tends to be different – the lava may shatter into millions of glassy particles. In Hawaii, where this commonly happens, the particles are swept up by water currents and later deposited as black sand around the coast.

EUROPE'S HIGHEST VOLCANO, MOUNT ETNA
ON THE ISLAND OF SICILY, HAS BEEN ALMOST CONTINUOUSLY ACTIVE SINCE PEOPLE FIRST STARTED RECORDING THEIR OBSERVATIONS OF IT 2500 YEARS AGO.

Its name comes from an ancient Greek word meaning 'I burn'. As well as several summit craters, Etna has numerous additional craters and parasitic cones on its slopes, all of which are capable of erupting huge quantities of ash, cinders and lava. Massive flows of basaltic lava, including both pahoehoe and 'a'a lava, have been a feature of many eruptions.

Etna's most famous eruption was in 1669, when it spewed around 830 million m³ of lava from a 9 km fissure on its southern flank. The lava streams overwhelmed the town of Nicolosi and six villages. The death toll was relatively low, because many inhabitants had already evacuated the area. Despite the constant threat of eruption, several thousand people live on the slopes of Etna, largely because of the fertile volcanic soil, built up from successive lava flows and ash falls over thousands of years. The soil supports vineyards and orchards, which spread across the volcano's lower slopes.

AGE: 2.5 million years
SURFACE AREA: 1560 km²
ALTITUDE OF SUMMIT: 3326 m
EARLIEST RECORDED ERUPTION: 475 BC
ERUPTIONS OVER PAST 3500 YEARS: 200
TOTAL KNOWN FATALITIES: 77

AIRBORNE HAZARDS

ALL LARGE VOLCANIC ERUPTIONS, AND EVEN SOME SMALLER ONES, BLAST BILLIONS OF PARTICLES INTO THE AIR ALONG WITH HUGE AMOUNTS OF GAS. The particles form when gas bubbles in the molten rock expand with such force that they break massive clumps of magma into many smaller fragments. As they sail through the air, these lava pieces cool and harden; in most cases they have solidified by the time they fall back to the ground. Collectively, the material that falls from the air is called tephra, and it can take many forms. The main types are ash, cinders (lapilli) and lava bombs.

Generally, the bigger the explosion, the smaller the particles. In the biggest, the magma fragments into pieces smaller than 2 mm in diameter, which produce clouds of ash. Medium-sized to larger ash particles gradually float down to Earth's surface, sometimes hundreds of kilometres from the volcano itself. As they settle, they form a dust-like layer over the landscape. Large ash falls

VOLCANIC BOMB An eruption of Mount Erebus in Antarctica in 1984 blew this lava bomb into the air. It was hollow when ejected from the vent and has since collapsed.

destroy crops, and when combined with torrential rain, they can result in dangerous mudflows. Wet ash on house roofs sets like cement and can lead to collapse if the ash is not removed. Although the ash is not usually poisonous, inhaling it can cause problems for people with weak respiratory systems.

Cinders, bombs and gases

Cinders are pieces of fragmented lava measuring 2–64 mm in diameter – some are ash particles that have become cemented together. In practice, cinder showers rarely cause injury or deaths and are less of a danger than ash, lava flows and volcanic gases. Unlike volcanic ash, cinders

HILLSIDE CLEANUP These young Icelanders are shovelling ash and cinders off a slope on the island of Heimaey. The airborne material was blown out from a volcanic fissure that suddenly and dramatically ripped across the island in 1973.

are too large to be breathed in, and a shower of small cinders would be no more likely to cause injury than a severe hailstorm.

Lava bombs are another matter. Classified as globules of lava more than 65 mm across, some can measure several metres. Although the larger ones rarely travel more than 500 m from an erupting vent, the smaller ones may fall to the ground several kilometres away. Volcanic bombs are a significant hazard and occasionally cause severe injury or death. In 1993, six people were killed near the summit of the Galeras volcano in Colombia when lava bombs unexpectedly pounded them from the air.

Toxic gases released during eruptions pose another type of airborne danger. Apart from water vapour, other gases may be given out, including carbon dioxide, sulphur dioxide, hydrogen chloride, hydrogen sulphide, ammonia and hydrogen fluoride. They can irritate lungs, eyes and skin, and some cause acid burns.

PYROCLASTIC FLOWS AND SURGES

FAST-MOVING MIXTURES OF VERY HOT GAS, ASH AND ROCK ARE A COMMON AND EXTREMELY DANGEROUS FEATURE OF ERUPTIONS. Called pyroclastic flows, or nuées ardentes (glowing clouds), they flow down the flank of a volcano with great force and speed, incinerating, flattening and burying trees, buildings and people. Typically, these deadly clouds flow down the mountainside at speeds of about 100 km/h and most travel for around 5–10 km. Pyroclastic flows usually consist of two parts: a 'basal flow' that hugs the ground and contains large boulders and rock fragments, and an ash cloud that rises above the main flow due to turbulence between the flow and the overlying air.

MONSTROUS FLOW On the Caribbean island of Montserrat, a collapsing cloud of lava fragments – a pyroclastic flow – bears down on a tiny hamlet at the base of the Soufrière Hills volcano in 1997. Within seconds, the houses and much of the greenery visible had been destroyed.

KATMAI: VALLEY OF TEN THOUSAND SMOKES

The largest volcanic eruption of the 20th century took place in June 1912 from a vent some 10 km west of the Alaskan volcano, Mount Katmai. The eruption, which measured 6 on the Volcanic Explosivity Index (see page 73), lasted 60 hours. Volcanologists believe that it discharged about 15 km³ of magma from a magma chamber beneath Katmai. As it was blasted from the vent (now called Novarupta), the magma turned into roughly 30 km³ of pyroclastic flows, which surged down into a valley to the north-west (below). An area of 120 km² was covered in ash up to 200 m thick. This would be roughly equivalent to burying central London in ash to a depth of one and half times the height of the London Eye. Following the eruption thousands of plumes of steam rose from the mass of hot ash as it cooled. It was still steaming in 1916 when an American botanist, Robert Griggs, first explored the region, naming it The Valley of Ten Thousand Smokes.

The most common cause of a pyroclastic flow is the collapse of the ash column following a large eruption. Normally, the ejected material heats the surrounding air, and the mixture then rises many kilometres into the atmosphere by convection. If the erupted plume fails to heat the surrounding air enough, convection slows and the material falls back down the flanks of the volcano.

Hot and cold surges

Even more dangerous than pyroclastic flows are pyroclastic surges, which contain a much higher proportion of gas to rock. This makes them more turbulent than pyroclastic flows and allows them to rise over ridges rather than simply travel downhill. Pyroclastic surges are also much faster than flows, reaching speeds of up to 350 km/h. They usually travel about 10 km from their source.

Pyroclastic surges can be either hot or cold. Hot surges, produced in the same way as pyroclastic flows, contain gas and steam at temperatures of between 100–800°C. Cold surges contain gas mainly below 100°C and are produced when magma comes into contact with a large volume of water – if the volcanic vent is under a lake, for example. The enormous destructive power of pyroclastic surges derives from the massive kinetic energy they carry. In addition, with hot surges, the temperature of the gas is lethal, while cold surges often contain large quantities of poisonous gas.

Ecological impact

The devastation caused by pyroclastic flows and surges can be immense. A flow from Mount St Helens in 1980 is estimated to have killed thousands of large mammals and millions of fish and birds. Not a single plant survived within the flow region – an area of 600 km². There was one benefit: the devastation gave ecologists a unique opportunity to study how ecosystems are influenced by, and recover from, such large-scale disturbances.

RIFT VOLCANOES

The Rift volcanoes' unique characteristics may be partly due to the magma that built them, which comes from uncommon rock types found in Africa's continental crust.

SOME OF THE MOST SPECTACULAR BUT LEAST-KNOWN VOLCANOES ARE IN REGIONS WHERE THE EARTH'S CRUST IS PULLING APART. Rift volcanoes occur at, or close to, divergent plate boundaries (see page 22) – either in continental rift zones or over mid-ocean ridges. Many of the land volcanoes of this kind are in the East African Rift System.

The Rift System (see pages 24-25) splits into two main branches. The eastern Rift Valley extends from Eritrea south to Mozambique. The shorter western branch runs from southern Sudan to western Tanzania. These two regions contain more than 50 large volcanoes and many smaller ones, many of them erupting highly fluid lava. Their unique characteristics may be partly due to the magma that built them, which comes from uncommon rock types found in Africa's continental crust.

Mountain of God

In north-eastern Tanzania rises Ol Doinyo Lengai ('Mountain of God' in the language of the Masai people), the only volcano in the world that erupts a type of lava called

LAVA LAKE A solid black crust often forms over the lava in the crater at the summit of Erta Ale in Ethiopia (opposite). In places, it is punctuated with plumes of fiery hot, red, liquid lava.

BIZARRE SUMMIT Grotesque lava formations like this are found all over the summit crater of Ol Doinyo Lengai in Tanzania. They are a result of the unique type of lava from which the volcano is formed.

natrocarbonatite. This is the most fluid of all lavas – it runs over the ground like water – and also the coolest, with a temperature of about 500°C. Natrocarbonatite lava also has a strange appearance. During the day, it looks like black oil or brown foam, depending on the gas content; at night it glows a vivid orange.

Lengai is a composite volcano. At its summit is a bizarre-looking crater, measuring about 350 m across and filled with solidified lava. Its eruptive activity is usually centred on one or more small cones that formed on the flat crater floor during previous eruptions. For much of the time, eruptions take the form of streams of lava issuing out of holes or cracks near the base of the cones or fountains of lava from vents at their summits. No one knows how the various vents in the crater are interconnected or what causes lava to flow at any particular time. Every decade or so, this pattern gives way to more violent eruptions with larger lava flows and ash plumes.

Mountain that fumes

Ethiopia's Erta Ale (the Fuming or Devil's Mountain) rises more than 600 m from the Danakil Depression, the lowest point in the East African Rift System and one of the hottest, driest, most inhospitable places on Earth. At its summit is a large, elliptical crater, which contains two steep-sided smaller 'pit' craters. At the bottom of one of these is Erta Ale's most unusual feature – a fiery, circular lava lake, about 150 m in diameter, that has been churning and occasionally erupting for more than 40 years.

At times the lake is fully molten, its surface stirred by fountains of lava. During these phases it gives off a prodigious amount of heat and light – eye protection is needed even to look at it. At other times, a solid crust forms over its surface. This was the case in January 2005, when a Canadian adventurer, George Kourounis, became the first person to lower himself down into the smoking crater to walk on the lava lake.

SUPER-VOLCANOES

LAKE TAUPO, IN NEW ZEALAND'S NORTH ISLAND, IS A LARGE AND PEACEFUL STRETCH OF WATER, famous for its trout fishing. Looking at it today, few would suspect that it was the site of one of the most violent eruptions of the past 5000 years. In AD 180, a volcanic explosion blasted 100 km³ of rock, ash and dust into the air, turning the sky red as far away as China and even Rome. On the Volcanic Explosivity Index (VEI, see page 73), the Hatepe eruption, as it is known, measured 7 ('super-colossal'). It devastated much of the North Island, but caused no human deaths, as it happened before New Zealand was inhabited.

Massive though it was, this extraordinary event was by no means the biggest eruption the Lake Taupo region has experienced. Approximately 22 600 years ago, an explosion took place that was roughly ten times bigger. Known as the Oruanui eruption, it blasted an estimated 1170 km³ of material into the air, caused the

From the history of past eruptions and the volume of material ejected, super-volcanoes are known to be capable of radically altering landscapes and severely impacting the world's climate.

collapse of several hundred square kilometres of land and created the depression (or caldera, see page 68) that Lake Taupo currently occupies.

A violent history

According to geological sleuths, the Lake Taupo volcano has erupted a total of 28 times over the past 27 000 years. Along with a small group of other volcanic sites scattered across the world, it is regarded as a 'super-volcano'. This is a volcano that, from the history of its past eruptions and the volume of material they have ejected, has shown itself capable of radically altering landscapes and severely impacting the world's climate, with potentially disastrous consequences for life on Earth. Each super-volcano consists of a massive caldera that in the past has been the site of at least one mega-colossal eruption (VEI 8).

Another such super-volcano lies under Yellowstone National Park in Wyoming, USA. Few visitors realise that the park is part of an ancient volcanic caldera, beneath which lies a huge magma chamber, fed by a hotspot in Earth's mantle. The biggest eruption occurred about 2.1 million years ago. Another huge eruption happened 1.3 million years ago, and a third some 630 000 years ago. Since these eruptions have happened roughly once every 700 000 years, some geologists believe that another is due fairly soon.

The largest eruption of the past 2 million years occurred at Toba, now a beautiful mountain lake in northern Sumatra, Indonesia. When it exploded 74 000 years ago, it blasted 280 million km³ of rock into the air, creating an ash cloud that blocked out the Sun as the debris travelled round the world. The result was a cooling of world temperatures by some 3–5°C. Scientists monitoring the caldera believe that Lake Toba will erupt again one day.

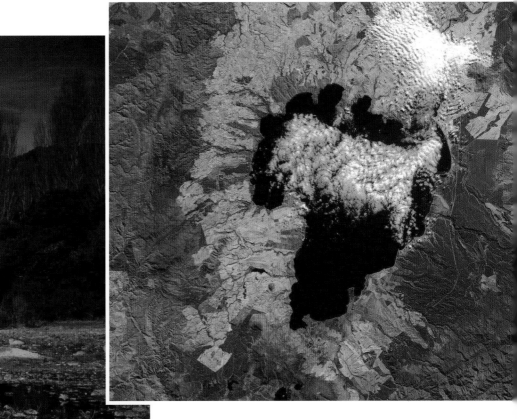

SLUMBERING BEAST Photographed in infrared by satellite (above) and from its tranquil shoreline (left), New Zealand's Lake Taupo gives little hint that it lies on top of a massive dormant volcano with a history of cataclysmic eruptions. Today, volcanic activity near the lake is restricted to hot springs and other geothermal features, from which New Zealand generates a significant proportion of its energy.

KILLER ERUPTIONS

WHEN MOUNT ST HELENS IN WASHINGTON STATE, USA, BLEW ITS TOP ON MAY 18, 1980, it unleashed a chain of events that made the explosion the most deadly and economically damaging volcanic eruption in US history. Rated 5 ('paroxysmal') on the Volcanic Explosivity Index (VEI, see page 73), it was triggered by an earthquake, caused by the movement of magma beneath the volcano. As the ground shook, a huge chunk of the mountain's northern slopes disintegrated and slipped away in the largest landslide in recorded history. Almost instantly, a mass of exposed magma exploded sideways out of the volcano.

The blast of the eruption flattened all standing trees within a fan-shaped area extending for 30 km, followed by a pyroclastic flow which incinerated everything over an area of 600 km^2. Within minutes, millions of tons of melted glacier ice from the volcano's summit, mixed with disintegrated rock and ash, created devastating lahars (mudflows). These surged down the local rivers, sweeping away bridges, trees and buildings. By the time the ash had settled and the lahars had slowed to a trickle, 57 people had died – most by incineration, burial or asphyxiation – and more than a billion dollars in damage had occurred.

EXPLOSION SEQUENCE A violent steam explosion (right) shakes Mount St Helens on April 12, 1980 – nearly a month before the main eruption. Below: A photographic sequence shows the mountain's transformation during the spring of 1980. By late March, volcanic ash had darkened its eastern slopes. After the eruption of May 18, the formerly graceful, snow-covered peak was a scarred scene of devastation.

MARCH 30   APRIL 10

APRIL 12

Disaster in paradise

For all the devastation, the 1980 Mount St Helens eruption was far from the most lethal of the 20th century. The most deadly of the century – and the third most deadly in recorded history – struck the Caribbean island of Martinique in 1902. On April 23, the island's active volcano, Mont Pelée, which had been dormant in living memory, suddenly began spouting sulphurous vapours near its summit. Over the next few days, the city of Saint-Pierre, some 4 km south of the summit, was showered in ash and rocked by earth tremors. As the eruptions intensified, water in the volcano's crater lake heated, eventually sending a torrent of scalding water down the flanks of the mountain on May 5. And this was only the beginning.

On the morning of May 8, the volcano erupted again, this time with a deafening roar. A large pyroclastic flow rolled down Mont Pelée's south flank at more than 160 km/h, reaching Saint-Pierre within a minute and burning everything in its path. Thousands of barrels of rum stored in the city's warehouses exploded, sending rivers of the flaming liquid through the streets. The entire city was incinerated and covered by volcanic ash. More than 26 000 people perished in Saint-Pierre that dreadful day, but at least death came quickly for them, within just a few seconds of inhaling the scorching fumes and ash. Scientists rate the eruption as VEI 4 ('cataclysmic').

MAY 31

JUNE 28

Death in the Sunda Strait

Nearly 20 years before the Mont Pelée disaster, an eruption caused the disintegration of a whole island – Krakatau in Indonesia. Lying in the Sunda Strait, between Java and Sumatra, Krakatau has erupted many times throughout history, but the cataclysm in August 1883 has achieved a legendary status. The volcano had been working up to its eruption with some serious explosions of ash since May 20. A series of four explosions that began on the morning of August 27 overshadowed these, culminating in a colossal blast that literally blew Krakatau apart. More than 25 km³ of rock, ash and pumice were spewed into the atmosphere or dispatched towards neighbouring islands and coasts in the form of pyroclastic flows.

Next came tsunamis up to 40 m high, which ravaged adjacent coastlines. They submerged many of the closest islands completely, stripped them of all their vegetation and washed the inhabitants out to sea. According to official records, 165 villages and towns were destroyed, 132 seriously damaged and some 36 500 people died. The explosion on the morning of August 27 is famous for being the loudest sound ever reported – people heard it in Perth, Australia, some 3100 km away.

The Tambora cataclysm

The eruptions of Mount St Helens, Mont Pelée and Krakatau were spectacular, but the explosion of Tambora in 1815 was even greater. Tambora ranks as the largest volcanic eruption in the past 1800 years – and the most lethal of all time for the estimated number of human deaths it caused.

Mount Tambora is a composite volcano on the Indonesian island of Sumbawa, about 300 km east of Bali. On April 5, 1815, after it had lain dormant for 5000 years, the local inhabitants were surprised by a series of loud bangs coming from the volcano and witnessed a moderate eruption of ash and cinders. Further small blasts continued for several days, until the evening of April 10, when the main eruption occurred. It is said that three columns of fire rose up into the air and merged, and the whole mountain turned into what one person described as a 'flowing mass of liquid fire'.

An estimated 350 km³ of ash and rock shot up into the atmosphere, and lava bombs up to 200 mm in diameter rained down. Lethal pyroclastic flows followed soon after, and there were heavy volcanic ash falls in Borneo, Sulawesi and Java. Some 11 000–12 000 people were killed directly by the eruption; a further 60 000–80 000 are estimated to have died subsequently from starvation due to loss of crops and livestock.

The eruption – with a VEI rating of 7 ('super-colossal') – had far-reaching effects. The ash it injected into the Earth's atmosphere lowered temperatures worldwide, and the following year, 1816, became known as the 'year without a summer'. In the Northern Hemisphere, failure of crops and livestock resulted in the worst famine of the 19th century.

The eruption that swallowed Pompeii

Possibly the most famous volcanic event of all time is the eruption of Mount Vesuvius, in southern Italy, on August 24, AD 79. It is best known for completely burying the Roman towns of Pompeii and Herculaneum, killing an estimated 3400 people there and in surrounding villages. Pliny the Younger, a future lawyer and author, who was about 16 at the time, witnessed the eruption from across the Bay of Naples. He wrote later that its main feature was a massive ash column, which resembled a pine tree: 'it shot up to a great height in the form of a tall trunk, which spread out at the top as though into branches.' Modern volcanologists estimate that the column would have been about 32 km high and give the eruption a VEI rating of 5 – the same as the 1980 eruption of Mount St Helens.

In Pompeii, about a third of the victims died inside their homes when roofs collapsed from the weight of ash that had fallen on them. Pyroclastic flows and surges, occurring towards the end of the eruption after many hours of ash falls and cinder showers, killed the rest of the victims.

THE TEN DEADLIEST ERUPTIONS

It is not only the people living on the slopes of volcanoes who have suffered from the many deadly volcanic eruptions throughout history. Large eruptions of ash can alter the local and even the world's climate, and smother and ruin crops for miles around. The resulting famine may claim thousands of lives. Lahars (mudflows) and tsunamis also have a devastating impact.

VOLCANO	YEAR	NUMBER OF DEATHS	MAIN CAUSE OF DEATHS
Tambora, Indonesia	1815	70–90 000	Starvation following destruction of crops and livestock by ash fall
Krakatau, Indonesia	1883	36 500	Tsunami
Mont Pelée, Martinique	1902	29 000	Pyroclastic flow
Nevado del Ruiz, Colombia	1985	25 000	Lahars (very fluid mudflows)
Unzen, Japan	1792	15 000	Tsunami
Laki, Iceland	1783	9350	Starvation following destruction of livestock by ash falls
Kelut, Indonesia	1919	5110	Lahars
Galunggung, Indonesia	1822	4000	Lahars
Vesuvius, Italy	1631	4000	Pyroclastic flow
Vesuvius, Italy	79	3400	Pyroclastic flows and surges; ash falls

ONE OF THE MOST DANGEROUS VOLCANOES

ON EARTH LIES IN THE DEMOCRATIC REPUBLIC OF CONGO. Mount Nyiragongo is the world's only steep-sided volcano that contains a lake of extremely fluid, red-hot lava in its summit crater. This makes it a killer. When the lava erupts it can flow downhill at frightening speeds, overwhelming villages and bringing instant death to anyone in its path. To make matters worse, it is close to a number of large population centres on the shores of nearby Lake Kivu.

Nyiragongo's dangers were illustrated on January 10, 1977, when the lava lake dramatically burst through several fissures in the crater walls. Within an hour, more than 20 million m³ of lava drained down the volcano's flanks at speeds of up to 100 km/h, killing at least 70 people – some reports say as many as 2000. On January 17, 2002, it erupted again. The nearby town of Goma was cut in two by a thick flow of lava and some 400 000 people had to be evacuated. The eruption killed 45 people and left 12 000 homeless. Nyiragongo remains active.

NYIRAGONGO

VOLCANO TYPE: Composite

ALTITUDE OF SUMMIT: 3470 m

WIDTH OF SUMMIT CRATER: 1.2 km

WIDTH OF LAVA LAKE: 300 m

ERUPTIONS SINCE 1975: 10

FATALITIES SINCE 1975: At least 115

LIVING WITH VOLCANOES

ONE IN EVERY 12 PEOPLE WORLDWIDE – AN ESTIMATED 500 MILLION INDIVIDUALS – LIVE WITHIN THE DANGER ZONE OF AN ACTIVE VOLCANO. Why don't they move elsewhere, safely away from the threat of volcanic eruption? The main reason is that volcanic ash is full of important nutrients, such as nitrogen, potassium and phosphorous. These enrich the soil, improving its ability to sustain crops, and the ash also improves the drainage of the soil.

People have been reaping the benefits of volcanic soil for thousands of years. The land around Mount Vesuvius, for example, is lush and verdant because regular eruptions over the past 4000 years have fertilised it with volcanic ash. The enriched soil supports a large grape harvest, which in turn provides employment for many in the local wine industry.

One factor has helped to make living near a volcano a bit safer today than it was at times in the past. Many of the more dangerous volcanoes, especially those located near large population centres, are scientifically monitored, and 16 of these – called 'decade volcanoes' – are given special attention (see pages 64-65). This does not mean that volcanologists can predict precisely when a volcano will next erupt, but they can often warn of an increased risk of eruption and give some idea of the likely character of a future eruption.

LAVA SAMPLING A volcanologist in full heat-resistant protective clothing takes samples of lava from Mount Etna in Sicily in 2001. Analysing changes over time in the composition of lava can reveal clues to a volcano's future eruptive behaviour.

Tremors, bulges and emissions

Volcanologists use a number of different methods to monitor volcanic activity. These include seismographic monitoring, the use of tiltmeters (instruments that measure ground deformation), surveillance by satellite and monitoring of gas and steam emissions.

Seismometers are instruments used to detect and locate moderate earth tremors under a volcano. These shallow earthquakes, which tend to become more common and intense as magma approaches the surface, are perhaps the most reliable sign that a volcano is about to erupt. Tiltmeters measure ground deformation close to a volcano or the development of a bulge on one of its flanks, which again is often caused by rising magma and may indicate an imminent eruption. Satellite surveillance is a novel, rather expensive, alternative to tiltmeters for measuring the same sorts of changes.

Another signal that magma is rising is increased emissions of volcanic gases, such as sulphur dioxide and carbon dioxide, from vents on the sides of a volcano – although this information is sometimes hard to collect, because the emissions are noxious to observers and can damage instruments. Volcanologists also take frequent samples of any lava and other erupted matter that a monitored volcano is producing. They analyse these, paying particular attention to their temperature and chemical composition. Sudden changes in either of these can indicate that an eruption is on its way.

Once a volcano has been thoroughly studied, geologists produce hazard assessment maps. These show the most likely routes of future lava flows, lahars (mudflows) and pyroclastic flows from a particular volcano, based partly on previous eruptions and partly on information gathered about its current state.

If the risk of an eruption rises to a significant level, the population will be advised to move away. In general, higher ground is less hazardous than valley areas. In the most serious cases, local inhabitants will be advised to evacuate the entire area within an identified danger zone.

PLANT COLONISATION *Plants typically start colonising new lava flows within ten years of an eruption. Here, scientists are measuring plant growth on the 40-year-old lava flows that comprise the volcanic island of Surtsey, near Iceland.*

Under the volcano

For landowners and farmers living in volcanic zones, the occasional eruption that produces a few centimetres of ash fall can be seen as a blessing. Yet the richness and productivity of the soil has to be weighed against the risks and dangers involved.

Scientists have analysed the causes of death as a result of the biggest eruptions of the 20th century. Their results show that the most devastating of these are pyroclastic flows and, in the case of volcanoes covered

THE MINOAN ERUPTION

Volcanic eruptions can affect the course of powerful civilisations. In 1600 BC, a gigantic Plinian-style eruption blasted from Santorini (also called Thera) in the Aegean Sea. Measuring 6 or 7 on the Volcanic Explosivity Index (see page 73), it was the second-largest eruption in recorded history, shooting some 61 km³ of rock into the air. It contributed to the demise of the Minoan culture – one of the great Bronze Age civilisations of the Mediterranean – and almost certainly upset the climate in the eastern Mediterranean and possibly the entire world.

Following the blast, believed to have taken place within an existing caldera, a

tsunami, 30–150 m high, smashed into the north coast of Crete, the centre of the Minoan civilisation, 110 km away. It is thought to have utterly destroyed the Minoan navy, many merchant vessels and numerous ports. On the small archipelago of islands that are the only visible remains of caldera today, a deposit of ash, 60 m thick, represents the fallout from the eruption. Buildings have been found under the ash, but no human bodies, suggesting that the Minoans who lived on Santorini at the time received some warning of the impending cataclysm. A magma chamber still exists under the islands and it is expected that one day another violent eruption will occur.

with substantial amounts of snow and ice, large lahars. Both are fast-moving hazards that cannot easily be escaped on foot or by taking shelter. In November 1985, the eruption of Nevado del Ruiz, a volcano in the Andes mountains in Colombia, was tragic proof of the dangers posed by lahars. It was one of the deadliest eruptions of the 20th century, leaving some 23 000 people dead, most of them buried by lethal lahars, which swept through the nearby town of Armero.

In addition, for people living in coastal locations near a dangerous volcano, there is a significant risk of tsunamis, and near some volcanoes there is the hazard of poisoning or asphyxiation from gas emissions. Heavy ash falls, as well as being a serious risk to health if the ash is breathed in, can also be lethal if they are allowed to accumulate on roofs that are not strong enough to bear the weight.

Although lava flows rarely kill, because in most cases people have time to get out of the way, big streams of lava pose a risk to property and agricultural land. Other natural disasters, such as earthquakes and tornadoes, also destroy homes and crops, but the owners can usually rebuild and recultivate in the same location. Lava, on the other hand, buries everything under tens of metres of hardened black rock and can obscure property boundaries. It can take years for land buried by lava to be made reusable, and the land often ends up being sold for a fraction of its previous worth.

Timely evacuations

Successful monitoring and timely evacuations can often avert a disaster. An excellent example occurred in 1991. Volcanologists from the US Geological Survey accurately predicted the June 15 eruption of Mount Pinatubo in the Philippines, allowing for the evacuation of a large area around the volcano, which had been dormant for so long that many locals did not realise the potential danger. The prompt action of geologists saved tens of thousands of lives, even though 300 people were still killed, mainly as the result of roofs collapsing under the weight of accumulated wet ash.

Another example of successful evacuation occurred in 1995–97, on the Caribbean island of Montserrat. Dormant for hundreds of years, Montserrat's Soufrière Hills volcano woke up in July 1995 with a series of intense earthquakes and steam explosions caused by the rapid heating of groundwater by rising magma. In subsequent months, a number of ash falls and lahars occurred as a result of further eruptions. By mid-November 1995, magma reached the surface and a lava dome began to form, threatening a pyroclastic flow if the dome disintegrated in an eruption.

On the advice of volcanologists, Montserrat's capital, Plymouth, and much of the rest of the southern part of the island were evacuated, saving thousands of lives – within a few months large pyroclastic flows hit Plymouth, burying it several metres deep in volcanic debris. In the end, many of Montserrat's inhabitants decided that the risks of living near a volcano outweighed the benefits. Of the 11 000 people who lived on the island when the volcano first erupted, as many as 7000 left over the next few years, about 3000 to the neighbouring island of Antigua and the rest to Britain.

NAPLES AND VESUVIUS One of the most densely populated regions threatened by a volcano is Naples and its surroundings, shown here with Vesuvius in the background. In the event of a large eruption, some 600 000 people will need to be evacuated.

ISLANDS
NEW

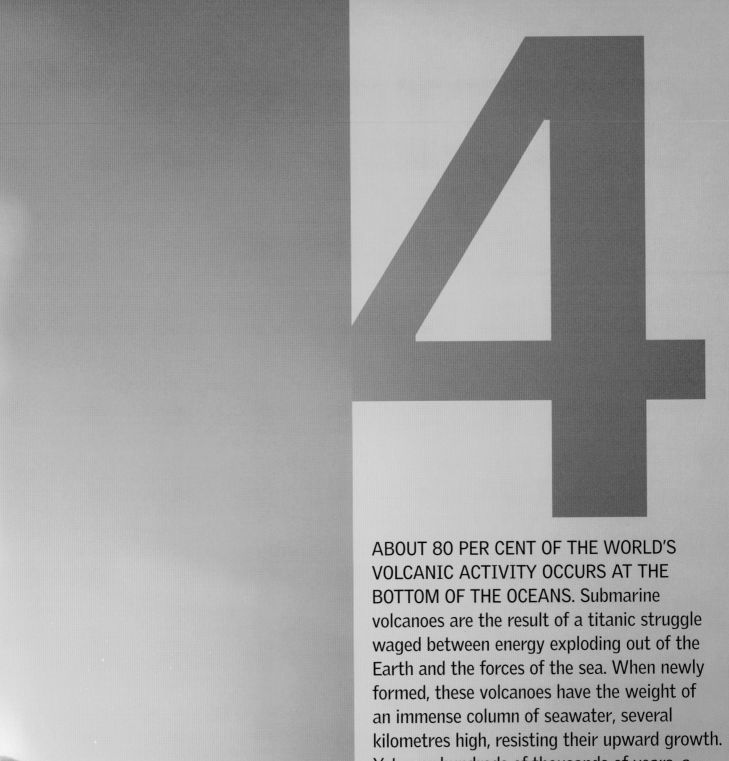

4

ABOUT 80 PER CENT OF THE WORLD'S VOLCANIC ACTIVITY OCCURS AT THE BOTTOM OF THE OCEANS. Submarine volcanoes are the result of a titanic struggle waged between energy exploding out of the Earth and the forces of the sea. When newly formed, these volcanoes have the weight of an immense column of seawater, several kilometres high, resisting their upward growth. Yet over hundreds of thousands of years, a few of them make their way towards the surface of the sea. Waves attack the soft ash and lava of a volcano, so for a long time its summit remains hidden underwater. But after vigorous successive eruptions, it may finally emerge into the air. If the volcano continues to produce lava flows, and if these harden, a volcanic island will be born, such as Isabela in the Galápagos (left).

SITTING ON A HOTSPOT

THOUSANDS OF VOLCANIC ISLANDS LIE SCATTERED ACROSS THE WORLD'S OCEANS, MOST OF THEM NO MORE THAN 30 MILLION YEARS OLD, WHICH MAKES THEM YOUNG IN GEOLOGICAL TERMS. Some are still highly active volcanically; others are now quiescent or extinct. Many lie over 'hotspots' – small, exceptionally hot regions at the top of the Earth's mantle that appear to remain in the same place for long periods.

Geologists believe that hotspots occur where 'plumes' of hot, semi-molten rock rise upwards through the Earth's mantle from the boundary between the mantle and the core. They have identified about 45 such hotspots around the globe, responsible for numerous islands and island chains, including the Hawaiian Islands, Galápagos Islands, Canary Islands, Mauritius and Réunion.

Hotspot theory

It was a Canadian scientist, J. Tuzo Wilson, who first proposed the idea of hotspots in 1963. Wilson noticed that in some parts of the world, volcanism has existed for tens of millions of years. His explanation was that some exceptionally hot regions must exist below the Earth's plates in these areas. According to his theory, the heat emanating from each hotspot partially melts the overriding lithosphere (see page 20), producing a continuous source of magma (molten rock). Being lighter than the surrounding rock, the magma rises up through the overlying crust. When hotspots occur beneath oceans, the magma erupts onto the sea floor, forming an underwater volcano. As this grows with successive eruptions, in due course it forms an island.

Wilson reasoned that as the tectonic plate lying over a hotspot gradually shifted its position, it would carry the submerged volcano or volcanic island with it. Eventually, it would transport the volcano beyond the hotspot, cutting it off from its magma source, and so preventing any further growth. But as one volcano became extinct in this way, another would start growing over the hotspot. Over long periods of time, whole chains of volcanic islands and seamounts (extinct submarine volcanoes) might form across the floors of the world's oceans.

Islands in a row

The best-known example of a string of volcanic islands believed to have been formed in this way is the Hawaiian Island chain. This extends for 2400 km in the central Pacific, more or less in a straight line, from the island of Hawaii itself in the south-east to Kure atoll in the north-west.

Starting in the south-east, the first eight islands – the youngest islands in the chain – are reasonably large. Beyond that, stretching out to the north-west, are a variety of smaller islands, atolls, reefs and submerged seamounts. Beyond Kure atoll, aligned in a significantly more northerly direction, is an extension of the Hawaiian Island chain, called the Emperor Seamounts. Both the Hawaiian chain and the Emperor Seamounts have formed over the past 80 million years as the Pacific Plate has moved over a hotspot in the central Pacific Ocean. The slight change in alignment between them is thought to have been caused by a small alteration in the plate's direction of movement, from nearly northerly to north-westerly, some 40 million years ago.

According to the hotspot theory, the volcanoes of the Hawaiian chain should get progressively older and more eroded the farther they have travelled from the

GALAPAGOS HOTSPOT A satellite image shows the two youngest of the Galápagos Islands, Fernandina and Isabela. Fernandina's single volcano, La Cumbre, currently lies directly over the Galápagos hotspot.

ONE HOTSPOT CREATED THE WORLD'S LARGEST MOUNTAIN, its tallest mountain when measured from base to summit and its most active volcano. Mauna Loa (the largest mountain), Kilauea (the tallest) and Mauna Kea (the most active volcano) are three of the volcanoes that make up the island of Hawaii, all formed by the Hawaii hotspot.

HOTSPOTS CAN MOVE. The hotspot that created Hawaii has stayed still for 40 million years, but over the preceding 40 million years it is thought to have moved slowly south.

MORE THAN 30 HOTSPOTS EXIST including at least 17 beneath the Pacific and 11 under the Atlantic.

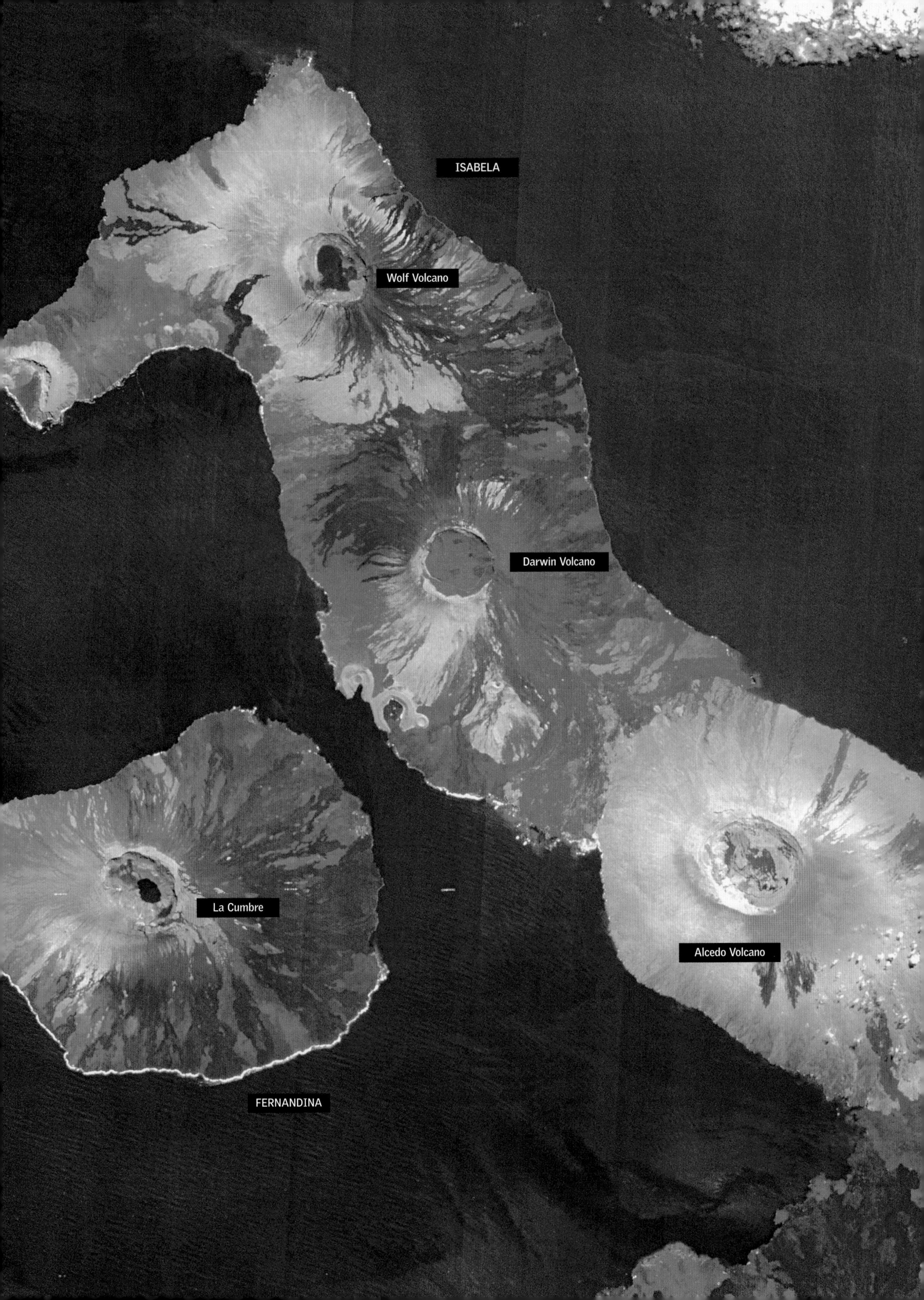

ISABELA

Wolf Volcano

Darwin Volcano

La Cumbre

Alcedo Volcano

FERNANDINA

HYDROTHERMAL CHIMNEYS *These formations were found on the submarine volcano, Loihi, the latest creation of the Hawaiian hotspot. They are evidence of past hydrothermal activity (plumes of spouting hot water) on the volcano's flanks.*

hotspot. This turns out to be the case. Of the inhabited Hawaiian Islands, Kaua'i lies the farthest to the north-west. Its most ancient volcanic rocks are about 5.5 million years old and heavily eroded. By comparison, the island of Hawaii itself – at the south-eastern end of the chain – is a geological baby, no more than 500 000 years old. In addition, Kilauea and Mauna Loa, the two huge active volcanoes that make up about half of the island, are continually forming new volcanic rock.

The hotspot theory also predicts that another volcano should be forming underwater south-east of Hawaii – and this also turns out to be true. Some 30 km south of Hawaii's south-eastern coast, and still 970 m beneath the surface, is the summit of the submarine volcano Loihi. The volcano has been intermittently erupting for the past 35 years and has already

risen to stand about 3000 m above the ocean floor. Loihi is believed to be about 300 000 years old; in another 100 000 years, it may reach the surface and start forming a new island.

The evolving Galápagos

In the eastern Pacific, some 970 km to the west of Ecuador, lies the Galápagos archipelago, another chain of volcanic islands. Consisting of 13 main islands, six smaller ones and numerous rocky islets, the Galápagos, like the Hawaiian Islands, formed over a Pacific Ocean hotspot – this one underneath the eastward-moving Nazca Plate. The oldest of the islands, Española, is thought to be 5–10 million years old, and the youngest, Fernandina, which lies directly over the hotspot, is still forming.

During his famous visit to the Galápagos Islands in September 1835, the naturalist Charles Darwin realised that the islands were geologically young. He noted in his book, *The Voyage of the Beagle*: 'Seeing every height crowned with its crater, and the boundaries of most of the lava-streams still distinct, we are led to believe that within a period, geologically recent, the unbroken ocean was here spread out.'

Unlike the Hawaiian hotspot, the Galápagos hotspot has not produced a simple linear string of volcanic islands. As would be expected from the motion of the Nazca Plate, the most active volcanoes are on the western islands. Although the easternmost islands are farther 'downstream' from the hotspot, some have young lava flows on their surfaces. Other islands are strung out to the north and south, and the overall pattern is one of several lines of volcanoes. This pattern is thought to be associated with where the islands lie in relation to plate boundaries. Unlike Hawaii, which lies in the middle of a plate, the Galápagos Islands lie just south of a mid-ocean spreading ridge, the Galápagos Spreading Centre. It is likely that varying activity at this ridge has been at least partly responsible for the unusual grouping of volcanoes.

Hottest hotspot

Other island and seamount chains formed by hotspot activity include the Marquesas and Society Islands, the Juan Fernández Islands and the Lord Howe Seamount chain in the Pacific, and the Canary and Cape Verde Islands, Tristan da Cunha and Fernando de Noronha in the Atlantic. Arguably the world's champion hotspot currently lies under the volcanic island of Réunion in the Indian Ocean. This hotspot has been active for at least 70 million years. About 67 million years ago, plate movements caused India to pass over it, and during this period the hotspot erupted an enormous volume of lava. Its remains can still be seen in a vast deposit of basaltic rock, called the Deccan Traps, in the western part of central India – the term 'trap' comes from the Swedish word *trappa*, meaning 'stair', and refers to the step-like contours of the landscape.

As the Indian Plate carried on moving in a north-easterly direction over the hotspot, more volcanic centres were created. The Laccadive, Maldive and Chagos Islands are built on former volcanoes created by the Réunion hotspot 60–45 million years ago. After a period of quiescence, it became active again about 10 million years ago and created yet more volcanic islands, including Rodrigues Island and Mauritius. Piton des Neiges and Piton de la Fournaise, which make up Réunion, are the youngest volcanoes the hotspot has created, both during the past 5 million years. Piton des Neiges is extinct; Piton de la Fournaise is one of the world's most active volcanoes.

> **Arguably the world's champion hotspot lies under Réunion in the Indian Ocean, which has been active for at least 70 million years. Piton des Neiges and Piton de la Fournaise on Réunion are the youngest volcanoes it has created, both during the past 5 million years.**

CRESCENT ISLE Molokini is all that remains of a volcano that erupted out of the waters above the Hawaiian hotspot some 250 000 years ago. The island, comprising the rim of a partly submerged crater, is slowly sinking beneath the waves, as it succumbs to the erosive power of the ocean.

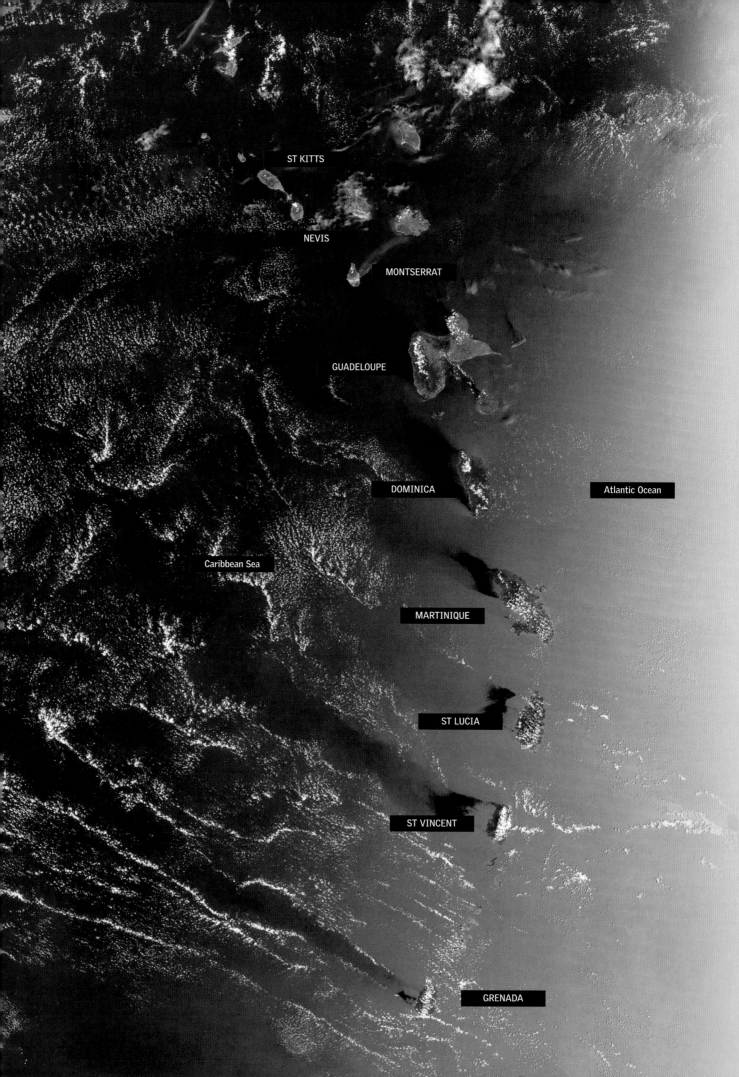

VOLCANIC ISLAND ARCS

NOT ALL VOLCANIC ISLANDS ARE CREATED BY HOTSPOTS. They can also emerge along the boundaries where plates meet and converge, the edge of one plate sliding beneath the edge of its neighbour. At a depth of about 100 km within the Earth, water escapes from the subducted (descending) plate and lowers the melting point of the rock in the adjacent regions of the Earth's mantle. As a result, large volumes of magma form and rise through the overlying lithosphere to the surface. The resulting volcanoes erupt on the sea floor, typically at a distance of about 200 km from the deep-sea trenches that mark the plate boundaries.

The underwater volcanoes in these situations are always arranged in a gentle curve or arc on the sea floor – the shape is a simple geometrical consequence of the Earth's own curvature. As the volcanoes erupt and grow upwards to the sea's surface, they form volcanic island arcs. The convex side of an island arc always faces either towards the open ocean or in the direction of the oceanic plate that is being subducted. Two of the best-known examples of volcanic island arcs are the 850 km Lesser Antilles arc stretching across the edge of the eastern Caribbean and the Mariana Islands arc spreading for 750 km to the south of Japan in the western Pacific.

An active arc – the Lesser Antilles

The Lesser Antilles volcanic arc lies close to a convergent boundary where the North American and South American Plates are both subducting under the Caribbean Plate. It extends in a graceful curve from near the coast of South America to the north-eastern corner of the Caribbean Sea (see left).

In the centre of the arc, the island of Dominica has no fewer than nine active volcanoes, although none of these has produced a major eruption in the past 500 years. All the rest of the islands possess a single active volcano, three of which – Mont Pelée on Martinique, Soufrière Hills on Montserrat and La Grande Soufrière on Guadeloupe – have erupted dramatically within the past century.

Geologists believe that it took upwards of 130 million years for the Lesser Antilles arc to form. The volcanic activity has not finished. At least one new island looks likely to form in due course – from an active and growing submarine volcano, known as Kick'em Jenny, which lies some 8 km north of Grenada. It currently rises 1300 m above the sea floor, with its summit crater just 180 m below the sea's surface.

Kick'em Jenny – whose picturesque name may be due to the rough seas common north of Grenada – is one of the most active volcanoes in the Lesser Antilles. The first known eruption

FORMATION OF AN ISLAND ARC At an ocean–ocean convergent plate boundary (see page 27), the edge of one plate consisting of oceanic lithosphere slides beneath the edge of another. Along the boundary, magma rises through the overlying lithosphere and forms volcanoes as it erupts onto the sea floor. As the volcanoes grow and eventually erupt at the sea's surface, the result is a volcanic island arc.

CHAIN OF ISLANDS A satellite photograph (opposite) reveals the graceful curve of the Lesser Antilles volcanic arc, stretching along the eastern edge of the Caribbean Sea. The convex side of the arc points out towards the open Atlantic Ocean.

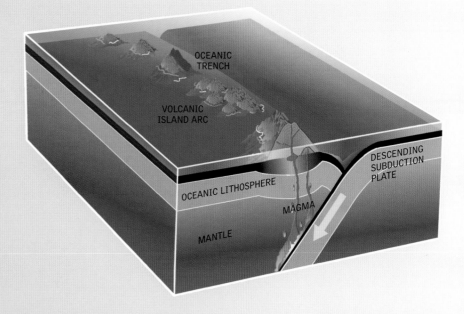

OCEANIC TRENCH

VOLCANIC ISLAND ARC

DESCENDING SUBDUCTION PLATE

OCEANIC LITHOSPHERE

MAGMA

MANTLE

occurred on July 24, 1939, and lasted for more than 24 hours. At one point, a column of black ash was shooting 300 m into the air out of the clear and tranquil waters of the Caribbean. The eruption also generated a series of small tsunamis.

Since then, Kick'em Jenny has erupted at least another 12 times, most recently in 2001. An eruption in 1965 was accompanied by earthquakes in the vicinity, and during an eruption in 1974, observers saw the sea above the volcano boiling turbulently. Recent exploration of Kick'em Jenny's circular summit crater found it that it was releasing a continuous and voluminous stream of hot and cold bubbles. This poses a hazard to any watercraft passing over it, as the degassing can significantly lower the density of seawater, which could lead to a boat sinking. Scuba divers from nearby Grenada occasionally hear deep rumbling noises that are believed to come from the volcano.

Activity in the Pacific – the Mariana arc

The western Pacific Ocean's Mariana Islands are another beautifully formed volcanic arc, rising from the seabed where the Pacific Plate dives under the Philippine Plate. Lying approximately 180 km west of the Marianas Trench, the world's deepest sea trench, the arc has been forming for around 42 million years and includes the islands of Rota, Tinian, Saipan, Anatahan and Pagan. Several of its constituent islands have active volcanoes. Three – Pagan, Anatahan and Agrihan – have had to be evacuated in the past 30 years due to the risk of cataclysmic eruptions.

The Mariana arc contains several large underwater volcanoes which, like Kick'em Jenny in the Caribbean, may develop into islands within the next few thousand years. The best-known of these, called Rota-1, rises 2750 m above the sea floor in the southern part of the arc. Its summit, called the

WHITE ISLAND This relatively young volcanic island is part of an arc that stretches for 2500 km between New Zealand and Tonga. It was given its name by Captain Cook in 1769, because it always seemed to be shrouded in white steam. The island is full of craters, steaming vents and boiling pools of sulphuric acid.

Brimstone Pit, is currently 535 m below sea level and is in an intermittent state of violent eruption, ejecting plumes several hundred metres high containing ash, glowing red lava, rock particles and molten sulphur.

About 150 km north of Rota-1, and north-west of Saipan, is another well-developed submarine volcano named Ruby, which rises about 2500 m above the sea floor. Its summit is just 200 m below the surface. In 1995, underwater explosions were heard coming from it, and local fishermen reported sulphurous odours, discoloured bubbling seawater and large numbers of dead fish in the area. There was also some evidence that the volcano's summit had grown significantly towards the surface during this eruption. In 2003, numerous plumes of hot water were detected rising from the volcano's summit and extending for several kilometres around it.

Emerging islands

Another dozen or so volcanic island arcs exist around the world, with new and emerging islands forming part of them. Most are found along the Pacific 'Ring of Fire' (see pages 30-31), including the Aleutian Islands in the northern Pacific; the Kuril Islands in the north-western Pacific; the main islands of Japan itself; the Japanese Izu, Volcano and Ryukyu Islands; and the Solomon Islands, Vanuatu and the Tofua volcanic arc of Tonga in the south-western Pacific.

Examples of new and emerging islands include Bogoslof Island and Fire Island in the Aleutian chain, which rose out of the sea in 1796 and 1883, respectively. Among the southernmost Ryukyu Islands lies a submarine volcano called Iriomote-jima, which had a major eruption in 1924. It produced vast rafts and blocks of pumice, which currents carried along both east and west coasts of Japan's main islands. Also part of Japan, the Volcano Islands contain numerous submarine volcanoes with summits close to the surface, including Minami-Hiyoshi and Fukutoku-Okanoba (see page 105). Farther south, the Solomon Islands are home to a 'now you see it, now you don't' volcanic island called Kavachi (see page 107), which appears temporarily above the surface and then disappears again – it has done so at least nine times since 1939. In the South Pacific, Tonga's Tofua volcanic arc includes several submarine volcanoes that occasionally form similar ephemeral islands.

CHILD OF KRAKATAU

The Sunda arc stretches for 3000 km across the Indian Ocean, where the Australasian Plate sinks beneath the Eurasian Plate. Its volcanoes created the Indonesian islands of Sumatra, Java, Bali and Flores. It also includes the small island of Anak Krakatau ('child of Krakatau'), which emerged from the sea less than 80 years ago, from the crater left when its parent, Krakatau, was blown out of existence (see page 88). Anak Krakatau has been a good laboratory for scientists studying the development of new ecosystems. All its plants came from seeds that arrived during the past 80 years. They are mainly clumped on its eastern side where loose ash and volcanic sand cover the ground. The majority are grasses, herbs and ferns, whose seeds have blown in on the wind, and coconuts, shrubs and ground vines, whose seeds probably floated ashore.

AN ISLAND IS BORN

MID NOVEMBER 1963

BY FAR THE MOST FAMOUS NEW ISLAND OF THE 20TH CENTURY IS SURTSEY, NAMED AFTER THE FIRE GOD, SURTR, FROM NORSE MYTHOLOGY. It appeared off Iceland in 1963. On November 14, fishermen noticed a plume of smoke rising from the open sea, about 33 km off Iceland's south coast. On investigating further, they encountered explosions at the surface giving off columns of black ash – a volcanic eruption was in progress.

Within a few days, an island some 500 m long and 50 m high, had formed, composed mainly of cinders and scoria

LATE NOVEMBER 1963

Situated above a hotspot close to the Mid-Atlantic ridge, the volcano that gave rise to Surtsey Island is believed to have grown from the sea floor to the surface in a matter of a few days.

BIRTH OF AN ISLAND Surtsey Island off Iceland was photographed in the first few days after its birth (left), two weeks later (above) and some 40 years later (right).

bubble-filled volcanic rocks). The early phases of the eruption were highly explosive, due to the interaction of hot magma and seawater. Closely spaced explosions produced dark clouds of ash and steam, shooting a few hundred metres into the air. Sometimes, the plumes extended up to 10 km above the growing island.

Rising from the ocean floor

The volcano that gave rise to Surtsey lies above a hotspot close to the Mid-Atlantic Ridge. It is believed to have grown from the sea floor, at a depth of 130 m, to the surface in a matter of a few days. By early 1964, Surtsey had reached such a size that seawater could no longer easily reach the volcanic vents, and the volcanic activity became much less explosive. Instead, lava flows started forming. These resulted in a hard cap of erosion-resistant rock forming on top of the loose cinders and scoria, saving the island from being rapidly washed away. After about 1 km^3 of lava had been spewed out, the eruption finally came to an end in June 1967, by which time Surtsey had reached its maximum area of 2.7 km^2 – its maximum height was 174 m above sea level. Since 1967, Surtsey has been shrinking, despite its erosion-resistant upper layer, and is already down to half its original size.

It has been of great interest to botanists and other biologists, who have studied how life gradually established itself on what was a totally barren island. The first life included lichens and mosses, which appeared within two years of the original eruption. These now cover much of the island. Within another 20 years, ten species of plant had colonised the island. As birds began nesting on Surtsey, their droppings enriched the soil, and more plants were able to survive. Some 40 years after the island's formation, about 30 plant species had become established, and new ones continue to arrive. The bird species now regularly found on Surtsey include puffins, guillemots, fulmars and various gulls.

An ephemeral island

The birth of a volcanic island is a dramatic sight, accompanied by clouds of steam and ash, but the island that forms will not necessarily be long-lived. Whether or not it lasts depends largely on the type of material erupted. The frequency of eruptions and the strength of local waves and currents are also important.

For a long-lasting island to form, there needs to be a persistent and vigorous series of eruptions over several decades. It helps if a large part of the volcano's magma is erupted as molten lava, which binds together loose rocks, cinders and ash as it solidifies, creating a sizeable, tough, wave-resistant mass of rock. More often, eruptions persist for only a few weeks or months, and the island that forms consists mainly of ash, small rocks and cinders. Generally, these islands are eroded and washed away within a few months or perhaps decades, and so become known as ephemeral islands. Although Surtsey has now been around for some 45 years, it is considered an ephemeral island, as it is not expected to have a total lifespan of much more than 250 years, a mere 'blink of an eye' in geological terms.

Now you see it, now you don't

In many cases, the summit of a submarine volcano appears intermittently at the surface and then disappears again over several centuries or decades, producing a series of ephemeral islands. These islands, spaced apart in time rather than location, often possess a single name even though their various incarnations may look quite different from one other.

Possibly the longest running example of this type of 'hide-and-seek' island lies in the Mediterranean, 30 km south-west of Sicily. Known for the past 170 years as Ferdinandea, it made its first recorded appearance in 250 BC. Since then, it has reappeared and disappeared again four or five times. One of its most recent incarnations began on July 13, 1831, starting with a column of smoke rising straight out of the sea and the discovery of large

2003

FLOATING LAVA This raft of steaming lava appeared in Japanese waters in July 2005. It was near the summit of a submarine volcano, Fukutoku-Okanoba, which has produced several ephemeral islands in the past.

numbers of dead fish at the sea's surface. Within a few days, an islet had appeared with a pronounced crater that spewed forth ash and lava. The activity continued for six months and the island increased in size to cover an area of some 4 km².

A dispute soon arose over who owned the island. The British (who named it Graham Island), King Ferdinand II of Naples (who called it Ferdinandea after himself) and the French (who called it Julia after the month of its birth), all claimed sovereignty. The issue was never decided, because shortly after the eruption had ended, the island started to erode rapidly away, finally disappearing beneath the waves in January 1832.

Ferdinandea is now known to be the summit of a massive submarine volcano that rises about 400 m from the Mediterranean sea floor and has a base extending for 30 km. It has recently been named Empedocles after the Greek philosopher who proposed that all matter is made of earth, fire, water and air – all these phenomena being apparent in an erupting underwater volcano.

Ferdinandea made a brief reappearance in 1863, but its volcano, Empedocles, has now lain dormant for several decades. In 2002, earthquake activity led to speculation about a new eruption. To avoid a re-run of the sovereignty dispute, Italian scuba divers hastily placed a flag on the volcano's summit before its anticipated reappearance as Ferdinandea, but no eruption occurred and in 2006 the summit remained about 6 m below the sea surface.

Almost islands

Another regularly occurring ephemeral island appears in Tonga in the South Pacific. It is known as Falcon Island after the British vessel HMS *Falcon*, which first reported a new island there in 1865. New versions of Falcon Island, growing up to 6 km long, were formed in eruptions beginning in 1885 and 1927; another incarnation formed in 1933 but had disappeared by 1949.

Farther north, Fukutoku-Okanoba is a submarine volcano 5 km north-east of the small Japanese island of Minami-iwo-jima, in a volcanic arc south of Japan's main island, Honshu. Water discoloration is frequently observed around Fukutoku-Okanoba, and ephemeral islands formed several times there in the 20th century, most recently in January 1986, when a crescent-shaped island developed and lasted for two months.

KAVACHI

THE MOST PROLIFIC CREATOR OF EPHEMERAL

ISLANDS IS KAVACHI, A QUIRKY AND UNPREDICTABLE UNDERWATER VOLCANO IN THE SOUTH-WESTERN PACIFIC, CLOSE TO THE SOLOMON ISLANDS. Since it first exploded out of the ocean in 1939, Kavachi has formed new islands on several occasions, but each time the newcomer has disappeared beneath the waves again within a few months to years. Intriguingly, each time Kavachi pokes its head above water, it does so in a slightly different location – the explanation is that the volcano has a moderately broad, flat summit with several eruptive vents.

Kavachi, named after a mythical sea god, is situated about 30 km north of a convergent plate boundary where the Australasian Plate dips beneath the Pacific Plate. Its full name is Rejo te Kavachi ('Kavachi's oven'). During eruptive phases, it has been known to project ash and incandescent lava bombs up to 70 m into the air, while sulphurous plumes of steam mushroom up to 500 m high. At night, an erupting Kavachi produces a fiery red glow and the occasional spectacular firework display that can be seen by passing ships.

During island-forming phases, Kavachi gradually grows out of the water through the accumulation of ash and cinders. Because it produces few lava flows, there is nothing to bind these fragments together, and so once an eruption stops, wave action quickly erodes the island away. The summit may recede to 30 m below the surface before the next eruption forces another temporary appearance.

HEIGHT ABOVE SEA FLOOR: 1.2 km
DIAMETER OF BASE: 8 km
PHASES OF ERUPTIVE ACTIVITY
    SINCE 1939: 30
LARGEST ISLAND FORMED:
    150 m long, 15 m high
LAST MAJOR ERUPTIVE PHASE:
    2000-2004
LONGEST QUIESCENT PHASE:
    9 years

GUSHING
AND WAT

GAS ER 5

IN ADDITION TO EARTHQUAKES AND VOLCANIC ERUPTIONS, THE EARTH'S INTERNAL ENERGY IS RELEASED AT THE PLANET'S SURFACE in explosions of water and gas. The best-known examples are geysers. The continuous spray of scalding water from the rocky cones of Fly Geyser, in the Black Rock Desert, Nevada (left), results from a groundwater reservoir being heated by a deeper chamber of hot, molten rock. Other phenomena that send water, gas or mud gushing and bubbling out of the Earth include hot springs, fumaroles, mud volcanoes, exploding lakes and escapes of methane gas. They can be dramatic – and sometimes deadly. A different form of energy is unleashed on the Earth's surface when an incoming tide enters a narrowing river with such force that it pushes the river back on itself.

HOT SPRINGS AND GEYSERS

HEAT ENERGY AND LARGE AMOUNTS OF WATER COMBINE IN THE EARTH'S CRUST TO PRODUCE AN ARRAY OF SPECTACULAR PHENOMENA. The heat energy comes from molten rock (magma) within the crust – typically in volcanic areas associated with hotspots or near plate boundaries – and the water from rain or melted snow. The panoply of effects created by the resulting hydrothermal activity (from the Greek *hydros* meaning water and *thermos* meaning heat) includes hot springs, fumaroles, geysers and bubbling mud pools. They make for spectacular scenery in places as diverse as Japan, New Zealand, Italy, Iceland, Chile and the United States.

Springs and pools

A hot spring is the simplest and most common type of hydrothermal phenomenon. It occurs when surface water percolates down through the rocks in the crust until it encounters a source of heat. As the water warms up, it becomes less dense, which causes it to rise again through an underground plumbing system of fissures, channels and chambers. When it reaches the surface it forms a pool of hot or warm water. Hot springs occur on all continents, and even at the bottom of the ocean, although their distribution tends to be quite localised – for example, in the USA they are found mainly in the western states.

In volcanic zones, underground water is heated through contact with hot rocks surrounding a magma chamber, typically a few kilometres beneath the surface. This may be an active magma chamber (filled with molten rock at a temperature of around 1000°C) or one containing recently solidified rock that is still extremely hot. In these cases, the water is heated close to its normal boiling point (100°C). If the water is under pressure, its temperature can rise above boiling point without boiling – a phenomenon known as superheating. Either way, the water that emerges at the surface usually has a temperature close to 100°C. People have been seriously burned or even killed by mistakenly or accidentally entering these springs.

In non-volcanic areas, hot springs result from water that has met hot rock by percolating deeper into the crust. At a depth of 12 km, rock has a temperature of about 300°C, and at a depth of 80 km, about 650°C. Water coming up from these depths cools on its route to the surface, so the pools of surface water that form in this way are usually warm rather than hot.

All hot springs produce heated surface water continuously and at a fairly constant rate. They vary from minuscule seeps to strong streams, each with a characteristic flow rate. Some particularly productive hot springs include Deildartunguhver in Iceland, which has a flow rate of 180 litres per second and a temperature of 97°C, and three large hot springs near Bajawa in Indonesia that collectively yield more than 450 litres per

GIANT SPOUTS Two geysers – the Prince of Wales Feathers Geyser (on the left) and Pohutu Geyser (right) – erupt in unison at the Whakarewarewa Thermal Reserve, New Zealand. They can blow steam and superheated water more than 30 m into the air.

HYDROTHERMAL FEATURES
The type of feature depends on the situation of the water below ground. Where heated water rises to the surface unhindered, it forms a hot spring. In places where the water supply is limited, a steam vent, or fumarole, forms. If mineral deposits line the water channels, forming constrictions, pressure results in the intermittent bursts of water and steam characteristic of geysers. Where rock is dissolved by steam and other gases, mud pools form.

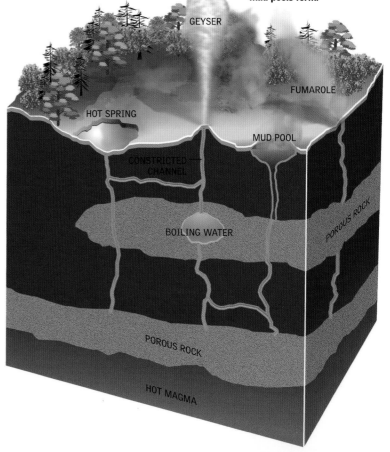

GEYSER

FUMAROLE

HOT SPRING

MUD POOL

CONSTRICTED CHANNEL

BOILING WATER

POROUS ROCK

POROUS ROCK

HOT MAGMA

second. A complex of thousands of springs at Beppu in Japan churn out almost 1600 litres of hot water per second.

On its journey through the underlying rock, heated water leaches out minerals. As the water cools at the surface, the dissolved minerals precipitate out of the water again to form hard deposits around the sides and edges of the spring's flow channels and pools. These deposits can form spectacular shapes, such as the travertine terracing at Mammoth Hot Springs in Wyoming, USA. Some exhibit extraordinary colours, such as the vermilion deposits of arsenic sulphide at the Champagne Pool in Wai-O-Tapu, New Zealand. Mats of algae and bacteria living in a hot pool can also contribute a range of bright hues.

A rush of steam

In some areas, where the amount of water in the ground is limited, the water heated at depth all turns to steam on its way to the surface. Instead of a pool of water forming at the surface, all that develops is a hole in the ground with steam rising out of it, often accompanied by a rushing sound. These holes are called fumaroles or steam vents, and they usually emit additional volcanic gases, such as carbon dioxide, hydrogen sulphide and sulphur dioxide. Fumaroles that emit sulphurous gases are sometimes called solfatara, from an Italian word *solfo*, meaning

A RELAXING HOT BATH At the Yudanka hot springs in Japan, macaques as well as humans enjoy bathing in the warm, mineral-rich waters.

sulphur. If hydrogen sulphide is present, it usually produces a smell of rotten eggs and may also react with oxygen in the air to produce elemental sulphur – this accounts for the bright yellow sulphur deposits that are often seen in hydrothermal areas.

Fumaroles may persist for decades or centuries if they are above a persistent heat source. Many are found on the sides or in the craters of volcanoes. One of the highest concentrations of fumaroles in the world – around 4000 in total – is in Yellowstone National Park. For those who can stand the smell of rotten eggs, Solfatara, near Naples in southern Italy, is another excellent location for viewing both fumaroles and hot springs. Its most prominent fumarole is called Bocca Grande ('large mouth') – the ancient Romans believed that this hot, steamy, foul-smelling vent marked the entrance to the dwelling of Vulcan, the God of Fire, although the poet Virgil speculated that it might be the entrance to Hell.

Bubbling mud pools

The combination of steam, hydrogen sulphide gas and oxygen in a fumarole will sometimes react to produce not just sulphur but also some dilute sulphuric acid. In areas where the ground is wet, this may dissolve the rocks surrounding the vent and turn them into a viscous, often bubbling, brown or grey slurry, called a mud pool or mudpot. Some of the most spectacular mud pools, looking something like huge ridged pancakes on a moonscape, are at Whakarewarewa Thermal Reserve, near Rotorua on New Zealand's North Island.

A variant on the mudpot or pool is the 'paint pot'. This is a mud pool in which the mud is tinged yellow, red or pink, usually

BLING MUD Mud literally boils in this pool
/ai-O-Tapu, a hydrothermal area in New
und. The mud is produced by dilute
uric acid – formed from a rising plume
t steam and hydrogen sulphide gas –
lving the surface rocks.

due to the presence of sulphur or iron compounds in the rock from which the slurry has formed. The thickness of the mud in a mud or paint pot changes with seasonal variations in the level of the water table.

The temperature of the mud varies from around 80–90°C down to a temperature at which people can wallow in it. In a hot and active pool, the mud churns and bubbles quite violently, and lumps of clay are occasionally squirted for some distance beyond the pool's edge. Over time, this can build up a distinct rim around the pool that can reach a height of a metre or more.

GEYSERS

THESE EXTRAORDINARY NATURAL FOUNTAINS ARE AMONG THE WORLD'S MOST SPECTACULAR AND UNUSUAL GEOLOGICAL PHENOMENA. Their violent eruptions shoot boiling-hot water, often accompanied by copious amounts of steam, for hundreds of metres into the sky. They are also rare – there are less than 1000 known active geysers worldwide, and more than 85 per cent of these are in just four fairly small regions. About 510 have been counted in Yellowstone National Park, Wyoming, USA; 38 at El Tatio Geyser field in northern Chile; 25 in Iceland and about 50 in the Taupo volcanic zone of North Island, New Zealand.

Unlike hot springs, which produce hot water steadily, geysers release it in intermittent bursts. While most geyser eruptions last for only a few minutes, some persist for days. Others erupt violently, and then do nothing for months or years.

Water under pressure

Like hot springs, geysers occur in areas where there is an underground heat source and an abundant and persistent supply of water. The crucial difference is in the underground plumbing. In a hot spring, water can flow freely to the surface from the various underground chambers and channels, so no pressure builds up within the system. In contrast, a geyser has a narrowed, constricted area near the top of the plumbing system, which blocks or restricts the flow of water, periodically causing a significant increase in pressure within the system.

Pressure builds up because the underground channels in a geyser are lined with a material called geyserite. This consists mainly of silicon dioxide that has been dissolved out of the rock by chemicals in the water, then deposited on the walls of the geyser's plumbing system. It eventually seals the lining of the system so pressure cannot leak out into the surrounding sand or loose gravel of the geyser field.

As pressure builds within a geyser, the water sealed inside the system is prevented from changing into steam. Its temperature continues to rise, reaching as high as 250°C – far above the normal boiling point. Eventually, water trapped in the constricted area at the top can no longer withstand the pressure and is blasted out. As this happens, the pressure a little farther down the system falls, allowing some hot water to turn into steam, which then rapidly expands. This sustains the eruption, which continues until the pressure in the geyser has dropped close to zero. The whole cycle then starts again.

There are two main varieties of geyser – cone types and fountain types. In a cone geyser, the geyserite forms a cone-shaped nozzle at the surface. This helps direct the flow of water in an eruption, rather like the nozzle of a fireman's hose. Most cone geysers shoot a continuous column of water straight up to a considerable height. In a fountain geyser, the surface opening consists of an open crater filled with a pool of water. During an eruption, water shoots out in different directions rather than in a single column.

Geysers galore

Yellowstone National Park is home to more than half the world's geysers, and is the best place to see not just the largest number, but also the widest variety of these spectacular phenomena. It is estimated that every day, Yellowstone's geysers release an amazing 300 million litres of hot water in eruptions.

By far the most famous geyser in Yellowstone is Old Faithful, which got its name because its eruptions are fairly regular. Old Faithful is a cone-type geyser with an average interval between eruptions of about 90 minutes, although the interval can vary either side of this. The typical eruption height of the geyser is about 40 m, and its eruption time is about three minutes. By analysing its geyserite deposits, scientists have estimated that Old Faithful is roughly 300 years old.

An older Yellowstone geyser is Castle Geyser, so called because the shape of its large cone resembles a castle. It is thought to be the oldest in the world: carbon-dating techniques indicate that it is somewhere between 5000 and 15 000 years old. Despite its old age, Castle still gives spectators a good show, erupting for about 20 minutes every 11 to 13 hours.

PRESSURE BUILD-UP

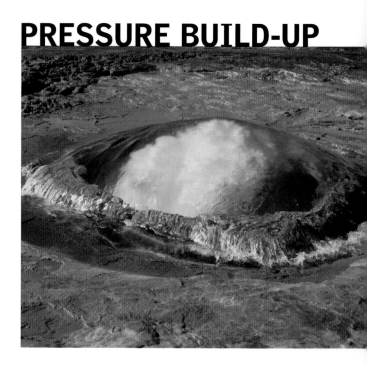

Changing geysers

No geyser stays the same forever. The dynamics of the hydrothermal systems that drive them continuously evolve. Yellowstone's Porkchop Geyser was originally a small hot spring that erupted only occasionally. Slowly, it sealed itself closed with geyserite, causing a build-up of pressure in its underground plumbing system. In 1985 it began to erupt continuously, but by 1989 the increase in pressure between eruptions became too great and on September 5 of that year it exploded. Porkchop then turned back into a small hot spring that is now slowly sealing itself up again.

Earthquakes can alter the functioning of geysers. In 1959, when an earthquake shook Hebgen Lake, Montana, near Yellowstone, many of Yellowstone's geysers started erupting, often for durations that had never been recorded before. While most of the geysers reverted to normal within a few weeks, some had changed permanently. Human activity, in particular the development of geothermal power plants, can also affect geysers. Geothermal drilling and power-plant development has led to the disappearance of whole fields of geysers in New Zealand, Iceland, Nevada and elsewhere.

PRESSURE RELEASE

STROKKUR GEYSER This Icelandic cone geyser erupts every 5 to 10 minutes. Each eruption is preceded briefly by the appearance of what looks like a large bubble at the geyser's vent, followed by a plume of boiling water that shoots 20 m high.

MUD
VOLCANOES

LESS GLAMOROUS THAN THEIR LAVA COUSINS, MUD VOLCANOES ARE CHANNELS THROUGH WHICH TONNES OF PRESSURISED MUD, salty water and oil are expelled from deep underground and released onto Earth's surface. They also spew millions of cubic metres of gas into the atmosphere – mainly hydrocarbons such as methane, but also some carbon dioxide and nitrogen.

A quite separate phenomenon from the mudpots and pools found in hydrothermal areas, mud volcanoes form mounds or cones of dried mud that range from 5 m to over 600 m in height and up to 10 km in diameter. Vegetation is normally absent around the cones because most plants cannot tolerate the high level of salt in the soil. Although mud volcanoes resemble lava volcanoes in some respects – occasionally they erupt explosively, hurling flames from the burning of hydrocarbons several hundred metres into the air – in other ways they are quite

MUD-MAKERS A stream of cold, viscous mud pours from the middle cone of a trio of mud volcanoes in Azerbaijan's Gobustan Reserve. Sights such as this have become part of the tourist itinerary in the country.

different. The mud is never hot, and seldom even warm as it emerges, and it comes from Earth's crust, not from the mantle.

Mud volcanoes form along fault lines in areas of weakness in the crust. They erupt when pressures deep within the Earth cause mud and water trapped underground to squirt to the surface. Pressure exerted on rock formations by deep gas deposits or by movements at plate boundaries can be an important contributory factor in setting one off. Approximately 1100 mud volcanoes have been identified on land and in shallow water around the world, in regions ranging from south-west Asia to Romania, Australia, Venezuela and Trinidad. An estimated 10 000 are believed to exist in the oceans, on continental shelves and abyssal plains. Sometimes they form islands and banks that can alter a coastline.

An estimated 300 mud volcanoes – about a quarter of the world's total – are in eastern Azerbaijan. Their eruptions are driven by a deep mud reservoir that remains connected to the surface even during dormant periods. Every 20 years or so one of them explodes with great force. Witnesses described an eruption that occurred on a hillside 15 km outside the Azerbaijani capital, Baku, one morning in 2001. After a big explosion a huge flame, several hundred metres high, spewed from the hillside. 'It looked as though an animal was trying to get out of the ground,' said one eyewitness. The flame was surrounded by dense black smoke, and tonnes of mud was thrown into the air. After five minutes there was another huge explosion, and the flame was replaced by smaller ones 10–20 m high. These could be seen from 15 km away and were still burning three days later.

In 2006, a huge mud volcano was triggered by gas-drilling on the Indonesian island of Java. It killed 13 people, submerged four villages, fields and factories, and rendered 10 km^2 of countryside uninhabitable for years. The deadly upwelling is thought to have begun when an exploratory gas well punched into a limestone aquifer 2800 m below the surface, allowing hot, high-pressure water to escape. It is thought that the flow will continue for many months – possibly years – to come.

EXPLODING LAKES

Some 80 km below the lakes pockets of magma still exist, and these are releasing carbon dioxide.

DURING THE NIGHT OF AUGUST 15, 1984, 37 PEOPLE LIVING NEAR LAKE MONOUN IN THE HIGHLANDS OF CAMEROON IN WEST AFRICA suddenly died, apparently from some form of poisoning or asphyxiation. According to eyewitnesses, an explosion had occurred in the lake, followed by the release of a cloud of whitish gas. Two years later, a similar and even more disastrous event occurred about 100 km away, at Lake Nyos. This time, more than 1750 people were suffocated, along with 3500 livestock, in villages around the lake. In fact, all animal life within a 25 km radius was killed. The normally clear blue waters of the lake turned a murky brown. A new term – limnic eruption, or 'exploding lake' – was coined to describe what had occurred.

By the early 1990s, following investigations into the geology of the area and the chemical make-up of the two lakes, a picture of what had happened began to emerge. Both lakes, which are about 200 m deep, lie within a type of volcanic feature called a maar – a

crater formed by interacting magma and water. Some 80 km below the lakes pockets of magma still exist, and these are releasing carbon dioxide. The gas dissolves in groundwater that feeds into the lakes, so both hold exceedingly high concentrations of the gas.

Much of the carbon dioxide is trapped at depth by the pressure of the water above, but any major disturbance – a landslide, perhaps, or a period of high rainfall – could destabilise the situation, causing some of the deep water to rise. As pressure on the rising water decreases, bubbles of carbon dioxide form, in the same way that they appear in a bottle of soda when the cap is removed. The bubbles rise rapidly, dragging the deep water towards the surface, at which point additional deep water is drawn upwards and de-pressurised. The result is a chain reaction causing a violent and sudden release of enormous amounts of carbon dioxide.

Deadly cloud

Although carbon dioxide is not poisonous, a large cloud of it is potentially dangerous because it is heavier than air and so tends to hug the ground. Researchers now think that up to 1 km³ of the gas suddenly erupted from Lake Nyos, possibly triggered by a period of high rainfall. Travelling at nearly 50 km/h, the gas cloud was channelled down surrounding valleys for up to 23 km. As it moved it displaced the air, asphyxiating all humans and livestock in its path. A similar course of events is believed to have happened at Lake Monoun, but the death toll was lower because the lake is smaller, with fewer low-lying valleys around it.

The magma pockets continue to recharge the two lakes with carbon dioxide, so scientists have developed a procedure for degassing the lower parts. A plastic pipe runs from the lake bottom to the surface, and water is pumped out at the top. As the deep water rises up the pipe, carbon dioxide starts to bubble out and more water is sucked in at the bottom, in a self-sustaining process. Degassing should reduce the level of carbon dioxide in Lake Nyos by around 99 per cent, and in Lake Monoun by 75 per cent, by 2012.

MUDDY WATERS Following the deadly events of August 1986, Cameroon's Lake Nyos turned a murky brown, providing a clue to the source of the catastrophe. A spectacular 50 m high fountain of water and gas now shoots above the lake surface, the result of the degassing of carbon dioxide from the lake bottom (inset).

METHANE MENACE

METHANE IS A SIMPLE, ODOURLESS CHEMICAL COMPOUND. Its molecules consist of four hydrogen atoms bound to one carbon atom. As the main component of natural gas – a fossil fuel found in natural oil and gas fields and in coal deposits – it exists in vast quantities within Earth's crust. As a component of a more complex solid substance called methane clathrate, it is also present in large quantities in the Arctic tundra and in sea-floor deposits. Methane gas is continuously released into the atmosphere from the bacterial decomposition of dead plant and animal matter, by mud volcanoes and from landfill sites. In addition, ruminant livestock release an astonishing 75 million tonnes of methane into the atmosphere each year as a by-product of digestive processes.

Methane is an important and useful fossil fuel, but it is also a potential menace. When mixed with air in proportions between 5 and 14 per cent, it is highly explosive. This poses a huge problem in environments such as coalmines, and when building near landfill sites, and has been the cause of numerous disasters in the past. Methane is also a potent greenhouse gas. If a massive quantity of methane were ever to be released into the atmosphere all at once, it could cause catastrophic

climate change. This type of event, a so-called 'methane burp', is thought to have happened in the far distant past, causing the extinction of millions of animal and plant species. In theory, it could happen again in the future.

Explosions and methane 'burps'

Explosions in coalmines from the accidental ignition of firedamp (methane-air mixtures) have taken an enormous toll of human life ever since large-scale coalmining developed during the industrial revolution. One of the earliest documented disasters from this cause occurred on June 18, 1835, at a mine in Wallsend, Northumbria: 102 miners died, including an 8-year-old boy. On December 6, 1907, at Monongah, West Virginia, a methane explosion caused the worst mining disaster in American history, with 362 dead. More recently, in February 2006, a methane explosion in a Mexican mine left 65 dead. Currently, China is the world's black spot for methane accidents and deaths in mines, accounting for about 80 per cent of the world's total, although it produces only 35 per cent of the world's coal.

The potential environmental menace from methane is arguably far more serious than its tendency to cause explosions. The amounts contained in methane clathrate deposits under the sea floor and in the Arctic are vast – 400 gigatons are locked into the frozen Arctic tundra alone – and these deposits are stable only within a certain range of temperatures and pressures. The type of global temperature rise currently predicted for the next 80 years – about 3°C – could cause a proportion of this clathrate to decompose, releasing more methane into the atmosphere.

Methane is a considerably more potent greenhouse gas than carbon dioxide, so a large-scale release would accelerate global warming, leading to yet more methane release in a runaway process. If triggered, this cycle could result in a degree of global warming far higher than predicted from the rise in carbon dioxide levels.

GAS EXPLOSION A tongue of burning methane-rich gas sprouts from China's Chuandongbei gas field during a sudden blow-out in December 2003. The explosion killed more than 200 people and destroyed surrounding vegetation (inset). Altogether, more than 40 000 people had to be evacuated from the death zone around the exploded gas well.

GLACIER OUTBURST FLOODS

ON SEPTEMBER 30, 1996, A VOLCANIC ERUPTION BEGAN FROM A FISSURE UNDER A MASSIVE GLACIAL ICECAP CALLED VATNAJÖKULL THAT COVERS A LARGE PART OF SOUTH-EASTERN ICELAND. Ice at the base of the icecap began to melt, draining into a lake contained within a volcanic caldera beneath the icecap. Over several weeks, more than 3 km³ of glacial ice melted and filled the caldera beneath the icecap. Then the icecap itself, which weighs billions of tonnes, started to lift, pushed upwards by the volume of water beneath. On November 5, the massive subglacial lake suddenly burst sideways through the rim of the caldera. Some water escaped beneath the icecap, while the rest blasted its way out through a fissure in the caldera's side.

The resulting flood obliterated several kilometres of roads near the Icelandic coast and destroyed a 376 m long bridge, causing damage totalling $14 million. With a peak flow rate of 50 000 m³ per second, it was temporarily the second-biggest

SUBGLACIAL ERUPTION
A huge ash plume rises fro
an eruption under Iceland's
Vatnajökull icecap in 1998,
threatening a jökulhlaup, o
glacier outburst flood.

river in the world after the Amazon, Within a matter of hours it swept countless tonnes of rocks and sediments to the coast, adding 7 km² to Iceland's total land area in the process.

Jökulhlaup!

Although the 1996 deluge from Vatnajökull is thought to be the greatest flood ever experienced in Iceland, similar events followed the eruption of other volcanoes under other Icelandic icecaps in the past. In fact, events of this type are so common in this northern nation that Icelanders long ago coined a term for them: *jökulhlaup*, which simply means 'glacier flood'. Although the term originally referred specifically to floods resulting from subglacial volcanic eruptions, over the years glaciologists have adopted it to mean any abrupt glacier-related flood. These floods are also referred to as glacier lake outburst floods, or GLOFs.

In parts of the world other than Iceland, the most common cause of a glacier outburst flood is the bursting or sudden drainage of a mountain lake that has previously been ice-dammed by a glacier. This can occur because of partial melting of the glacier; erosion of a glacial moraine (a pile of rock debris deposited by a glacier at its snout); a build-up of water pressure behind the ice dam; an avalanche of rock or heavy snow; an earthquake; or a large portion of a glacier breaking off and displacing the water in a glacial lake. Another possible cause is a cryoseism, or icequake – a type of tremor produced by sudden glacial motion, sometimes due to a thin layer of water from surface melt collecting under a glacier.

The incidence and risks of catastrophic glacier outbursts has increased markedly over the past few decades because of the retreat of glaciers worldwide – one of the results of global warming. This has greatly increased the number and size of glacial lakes in the world's high mountain regions. As remote mountain valleys become settled, more people and property are put in danger. While all countries with glaciers are susceptible to the problem, those identified as being at greatest risk include Central Asia, the Himalayas, the Andes region and some parts of the Alps.

In the Pamir Mountains of Tajikistan, a glacier posing a considerable threat is the 15 km long Medvezhi Glacier. Advances and retreats of this glacier have repeatedly caused the formation of lakes, followed by outbursts and floods. Of the 2674 glacial lakes in Bhutan, in the eastern Himalayas, 24 have been identified as candidates for glacial outburst floods, and from time to time one of them does burst. In October 1994, an outburst 90 km upstream from Punakha caused massive flooding and casualties in the city, and damaged the Punakha Dzong, the fortress that for many centuries was the seat of religious and political power in Bhutan.

The Andes are the site of the most deadly recorded glacial lake disaster of all time, which hit the town of Huaráz in the Cordillera Blanca, Peru, in December 1941. The town was destroyed and at least 6000 people died when a glacial moraine damming Lake Palca burst, allowing billions of cubic metres of water to cascade into the valley below. Recently, warnings have been given that a repeat of the disaster is possible. In the Alps there are dangers, too. In Italy, the 700 people who live in a village called Macugnaga have been at risk of flooding since the centre of the Belvedere Glacier on Monte Rosa began melting rapidly; the resulting lake is estimated to hold some 3 million m³ of water.

CARVED BY FLOOD Palouse Falls in Washington State, USA (right), is part of the Channeled Scablands – a unique landscape created by cataclysmic glacier outburst floods at the end of the last ice age.

ICE DAM

ONE GLACIER THAT HAS EXPERIENCED NUMEROUS OUTBURST FLOODS – WITHOUT POSING A PARTICULAR DANGER TO PEOPLE AND PROPERTY – IS THE PERITO MORENO GLACIER IN SOUTHERN ARGENTINA. This glacier descends from a huge icefield in the High Andes (the Southern Patagonian Icefield), with its snout terminating in Lake Argentina, the largest lake in Argentina. There, icebergs break off from its terminus and float away across the lake.

Over the past 90 years, the glacier has made several temporary advances across the lake, blocking off an arm known as Brazo Rico, which then becomes a separate lake. Because the ice dams off the new lake, the water level in it rises inexorably, sometimes up to 30 m above the level of the main lake. Eventually, after 6 to 12 months, the pressure on the glacial barrier created

ICE DAM BREACHED

GLACIAL DAM The satellite image shows the Perito Moreno Glacier damming off part of Lake Argentina, creating the Brazo Rico lake. Water flows into this from the surrounding hills (arrows). In 2006, water pressure blasted a tunnel through the dam (below left). Later, a section of the remaining ice bridge collapsed (below right).

LAKE ARGENTINA

PERITO MORENO GLACIER

BRAZO RICO

by the rising water causes it to burst in spectacular fashion, and about a billion tonnes of water are discharged in 24 hours. The rupture of the dam happens, on average, about once every four to five years, then the build-up begins again. Because the ruptures are recurrent, the area flooded by each outburst is well-defined and the actual timing of a rupture fairly easy to predict once an ice dam forms, which makes the Perito Moreno less dangerous than the majority of *jökulhlaups*.

Why ice dams collapse

Considerable amounts of scientific research have gone into investigating and explaining exactly why it is that glacial dams holding back mountain lakes suddenly collapse. The accepted explanation is that at the base of an ice dam, where water pressure is highest, melting causes minuscule cracks to develop in the ice (the melting point of ice decreases with increased pressure). Friction from water flowing through these cracks generates just enough heat to melt a little more of the ice and the

cracks enlarge. This creates a cycle of more water flow, more heat generation and further crack enlargement. Eventually, the lower part of the ice dam weakens so much that it can no longer support the pressure of the water behind it, and the water blasts a tunnel through it.

Timebomb glacier lakes

A number of glacier lakes have been identified around the world that are in imminent danger of bursting out from their glacial dams, potentially with lethal results. The largest and most dangerous is the Tsho Rolpa Glacier Lake in Nepal, located 110 km north-east of Kathmandu. At an altitude of 4580 m, it is dammed by a 150 m high moraine left by the retreating Trakarding Glacier. Due to the melting and retreat of the glacier, the lake is growing and now stores more than 80 million m³ of water. If the dam burst, the resulting flood would threaten up to 6000 lives, numerous villages, farmlands, roads, bridges and trails. To mitigate the potential for disaster, a system using satellite technology has been installed to warn people downstream if and when an outburst flood begins.

ICE BRIDGE FALLS

TIDAL BORES

THE TIDAL BORES THAT SWEEP UP SOME RIVERS RESULT NOT FROM FORCES WITHIN THE EARTH, but from gravitational interaction between the Earth and the Moon. Bores are a tidal phenomenon in which the leading edge of the incoming tide forms a wave that travels up a river against the direction of the downflowing current. As such, they are true tidal waves.

Funnelled water

Bores occur in relatively few locations, usually in places with a large difference (typically 6 m or more) between the maximum high tide and minimum low tide. A tidal bore occurs where the incoming flood tide is funnelled via a broad bay into a narrowing river. When the tide reaches a critical height, it forms a wave. The height of the wave rises and falls as it travels up river depending on the river's width and depth. Tidal bores take various forms, ranging from a single breaking wave front – effectively a shockwave – to a train of waves.

The world's largest and most spectacular tidal bore occurs at the mouth of the Qiántáng Jiang River near Hangzhou, China. It can be up to 8.9 m high (though more usually 3–4 m high) and travel at speeds of up to 40 km/h, sweeping past Hangzhou to menace shipping in the city's harbour and anything else in its way. No surfer has managed to remain upright on it for more than 11 seconds.

The *benak* (tidal bore) on the Batang Lupar river in Sarawak, Malaysia, has a claim to be the furthest-travelling of the world's tidal bores: the wave surges inland along the river for more than 68 km from its mouth in the estuary region of Pulau Seduku. The *benak* reaches a maximum height of 3 m and a speed of 18 km/h at the town of Sri Aman, about 28 km from the river mouth.

Tidal bores occur on large spring tides in several river estuaries in northern Brazil. Some attain heights of 3 m or more, travel at speeds of up to 30 km/h and can be surfed for several kilometres. The sport of bore-surfing has recently become highly popular in these river estuaries, sometimes providing the opportunity to ride a wave for 30 minutes or more.

The Severn estuary in England has more than 250 tidal bores a year. Some have carried surfers upstream for up to 10 km. Arguably Europe's most impressive tidal bore develops in the Gironde estuary in France. It becomes most conspicuous as it surges from the Gironde into its narrower tributaries, the Dordogne and Garonne rivers.

MOVING EARTH, ICE AND SNOW

6

LANDSLIDES, ROCK FALLS, ICE AND SNOW AVALANCHES, MUDFLOWS AND LAHARS ARE EXAMPLES OF ENERGY BEING RELEASED at the Earth's land surface. They are impressive, often terrifying, phenomena. And they all occur chiefly because the Earth's surface is not flat. On landscape features such as mountains, cliffs and canyons, loose material, including soil or volcanic ash, or a covering of snow or ice, possesses a particular type of energy – called potential or gravitational energy. Because of the location, the loose material has the potential to move downhill under the pull of gravity. When this happens, as in this snow avalanche in the Swiss Alps (left), the gravitational energy is converted into other, more dramatic forms of energy, with spectacular and sometimes devastating results.

LANDSLIDES

WHEN GRAVITY OVERCOMES FRICTION AND PULLS ROCKS AND SOIL DOWNHILL, THE RESULT IS A LANDSLIDE. These dramatic events can wreak huge destruction and, in the worst cases, kill thousands. That is what happened in the Peruvian Andes on May 31, 1970. Following a large earthquake, the glacier-covered northern flank of Peru's highest mountain, Huascarán, collapsed, sending a block of ice and rock, 1700 m long, 750 m wide and 750 m deep, crashing down into the valley below. As this disintegrated, the rock and ice mixed, forming an avalanche of mud that flowed for 20 km, burying the nearby town of Yungay and killing 17 000 people.

There are three main types of landslide – falls, slides and flows. A fall is a free fall of rocks or soil. A slide occurs when a block of material shifts downhill over a well-defined slippage surface, with little change to the original shape and form of the shifting material. A flow is a more diffuse, fluid type of movement that preserves none of the original shape of the displaced material. The Huascarán disaster was an example of a flow. Combinations of the three types can occur. A slide, for instance, may develop into a flow as the sliding material disintegrates.

The speed of landslides varies in terms of how quickly they develop and how fast they travel downhill. Falling or tumbling rocks accelerate downwards under the influence of gravity and can quickly attain speeds of hundreds of kilometres per hour. Flows can travel at anything from 50 to 250 km/h, depending on the angle of the slope and the type of materials present – those with an appreciable water content usually travel fastest.

Maximum slopes and triggers

Any mound or cliff of a particular material has a maximum angle of slope – it cannot be steeper than this angle – maintained either by friction or by the cohesive forces between its constituent particles. This is true of both unconsolidated material, including most soils, in which the particles are loose, and consolidated material – most types of rock – in which the particles are strongly bonded together.

ROCK FALL Some 30 000 tonnes of rock fell without warning from this cliff onto a coastal highway on the island of Réunion. Several vehicles were damaged and partially buried.

CREEP AND SOLIFLUCTION

Two types of downhill soil movement – creep and solifluction – occur on very gentle slopes and are extremely gradual, typically shifting just a few centimetres every year. Creep is a result of freezing and thawing. In winter, as the soil on a slope freezes, it is pushed up perpendicular to the ground surface. When the soil thaws again in spring, it drops vertically, ending up slightly downhill from its position the previous autumn.

Solifluction occurs where waterlogged soil slowly moves downhill over an underlying layer of impermeable material. It can happen in any climate where the ground becomes very wet, but most commonly takes place where the underlying ground is permanently frozen (permafrost). During warm periods, the saturated surface soil slides downhill over the frozen subsoil, lubricated by water or fine sediment at its base. This movement can occur on slopes as shallow as 0.5 degrees.

SLIPPED SOIL Triggered by an earthquake, this slide in 2001 started with a block of soil slipping down a steep escarpment at the edge of the city of Santa Tecla in El Salvador. The slide disintegrated into a flow, resulting in the deaths of more than 580 people.

Resistance to erosion plays a key part in determining a slope's maximum angle. Erosion-resistant rocks, such as granite, can form almost perpendicular cliffs, while softer rocks form gentler slopes. Another factor is the strength of erosional forces, such as wind and rain. In deserts, rock cliffs are quite common, but in areas where the climate is more varied and rainfall higher, slopes are more likely to be shallower and to consist of fragmented debris.

Much of both the consolidated and unconsolidated material found all over the Earth's surface is contained within slopes that are near their maximum angle of slope. If a triggering factor upsets one of the forces maintaining the slope, the result can be a landslide. An earthquake or volcanic activity, for example, may violently disturb the material in a hill or cliff, causing it to collapse to a more stable position. Other factors that may trigger a slope to collapse are if the frictional or binding forces between its constituent particles are altered by water, if its structure is weakened by erosion, or if additional weight is added to it in the form of buildings. Hong Kong – one of the most densely populated areas in the world – has a long history of landslides. Most have resulted from the effects of heavy rainfall on steep slopes weakened by the use of poor construction techniques.

The removal of vegetation is another factor. When a hillside is covered with many trees and other vegetation, the roots create

WET SOIL Torrential rain saturating the soil caused this hillside collapse in southern California in 2005. It damaged or destroyed 19 homes in Laguna Beach.

an interlocking network that strengthens the unconsolidated material; the vegetation also absorbs excess water in the soil. When vegetation is removed, the stabilising influences go with it.

Rock falls

Rocks most commonly become loose in a cliff through erosion following torrential rain or through freeze-thaw weathering processes. The latter happen when water flows into cracks and crevices in a mass of rock during the day, then freezes if the temperature drops sufficiently at night. Since water expands when it freezes, it forms a wedge that can eventually break off pieces of rock. Earthquakes can also trigger rock falls.

In most cases, fallen material accumulates at the bottom of a cliff as a jumble of rocks called scree or talus, but falling rocks sometimes dislodge other rocks and cause rock avalanches.

SLIDE AND SLUMP Following heavy rain in June 1993, a section of water-saturated cliff collapsed dramatically in Scarborough in North Yorkshire.

These can be sudden, violent and rapid, moving at speeds of up to 300 km/h. The largest rock avalanches result from the collapse of volcanoes, as when Mount St Helens erupted in Washington State, USA, in 1980 (see page 86).

Steep cliffs made of hard, resistant rock commonly collapse because of undercutting – the loss of supporting rock at the base of a cliff. Erosion by waves may cause this, as may badly planned construction work, which cuts away too much at the slope. Cliffs composed of softer material, such as clay, more often collapse as a result of saturation with rainwater.

Sliding and flowing

A common cause of slides of unconsolidated material is heavy rainfall or melting snow, which saturates the ground with water. The water both reduces the stability of the slope and also acts as a lubricant once the soil and rock have started moving. It may take weeks before enough water infiltrates a slope to cause a slide.

Mudflows (sometimes called debris flows) tend to be more destructive than slides. They consist of a mixture of water

THE SHASTA VALLEY

Thousands of mounds, hummocks, ridges and depressions corrugate the floor of the Shasta Valley in northern California, interspersed with blocks of lava, measuring tens to hundreds of metres across. This bizarre landscape is the result of a huge landslide that happened 300 000–380 000 years ago, following the partial collapse of a massive ancient volcano, possibly due to water-saturated slopes. The landslide had an estimated volume of 30–40 km³ and its debris extended for 45 km to the north-west of modern-day Mount Shasta. The deposits remain, along with numerous huge boulders of volcanic rock that lie scattered above them on the valley's western side. These are thought to have rolled down from the ancient volcano some time after the main landslide came to rest.

with soil or rock fragments and sometimes vegetation. Mudflows vary from viscous and relatively slow-moving slurries to highly fluid rivers of mud and are most often caused when an earthquake disturbs water-saturated slopes or glacier-covered mountains, as happened at Huascarán in May 1970. A lahar is an extremely dangerous type of fluid mudflow (see page 137), in which ash and pumice from a volcanic eruption mix with melted ice and snow, then flow rapidly down a mountainside.

Underwater landslides

Landslides also happen underwater, often on continental slopes – the sloping regions between continental shelves (the shallow marine areas around continents) and the deep sea floor. Causes include submarine earthquakes, hurricanes and the setting off of explosives underwater. Submarine landslides can occur on the slopes of oceanic volcanoes, such as the hotspot-generated volcanoes of the Hawaiian Islands and Canary Islands.

Imaging of the underwater slopes around some of these volcanoes suggests that they have repeatedly collapsed in the past. For example, blocks of rock up to a kilometre wide have been detected on the slopes around some of the Canary Islands. Some scientists believe that during a future eruption, the Cumbre Vieja volcano on the island of La Palma is likely to collapse and drop 150–500 km³ of rock into the Atlantic Ocean. This vast mass of material would continue moving underwater for 60 km before reaching the sea floor at a depth of 4000 m. If a slide of this size ever happened, it could trigger a tsunami with the potential to devastate the eastern US seaboard and the western coasts of Europe and Africa.

Ancient debris

When a landslide occurs in a region, such as a desert, with little subsequent erosion, the debris may stay visible for thousands of years. A spectacular example lies in southern California's Mojave Desert – the remains of a landslide, called the Blackhawk Slide, which happened some 17 000 years ago. It consists of a tongue-like sheet of material, 9 km long, 3 km wide and 9–30 m thick.

By examining the rocky debris, mainly broken-up limestone, geologists have worked out exactly what happened. The mass of rock originated 1200 m up in the nearby San Bernardino Range, where a block of limestone had been thrust up over softer rock strata. These softer rocks were subsequently eroded away, and one day the overhanging limestone mass collapsed into the canyon below. As it hit the canyon floor, it disintegrated to form a massive stream of rock debris, which then moved horizontally at 250 km/h. A few seconds later, this hit a ridge on the canyon floor and was launched into the air like a flying carpet of rock fragments. As this dropped, it compressed the air trapped beneath it to form a frictionless cushion less than a metre thick. As the slide spread over the desert floor, the cushion of compressed air on which it was floating became thinner, eventually permitting the rock debris to settle into its present configuration.

RIVERS OF MUD

SOME OF THE MOST DEVASTATING MUDFLOWS ARE FAST-FLOWING SLURRIES OF WATER MIXED WITH ASH, ROCK AND OTHER DEBRIS THAT FORM ON THE SLOPES OF VOLCANOES. Known as lahars, they resemble rivers of wet concrete, varying in width, depth and speed.

Small lahars may be no more than a few metres wide and travel at speeds of 10–20 km/h; larger ones, tens of metres wide, can move at a terrifying 100 km/h or more, ripping trees out of the ground and transporting boulders the size of houses. Their speed and power make them extremely destructive to anything that gets in their way. The lahars that developed after the eruption of Mount St Helens in 1980 destroyed more than 200 houses and 300 km of roads and smashed or damaged 27 bridges.

Any event that mixes large amounts of water or ice with volcanic material can trigger a lahar. A common factor is torrential rain falling on a volcano, loosening ash and other debris on its slopes. Others include the eruption of large amounts of hot volcanic ash onto a glacier or snowfield at the top of a volcano, or an eruption from a water-filled crater. Lahars have been known to occur when pyroclastic flows (see page 80) run into mountain lakes, or when the glacier-covered flanks of a volcano disintegrate after an eruption or earthquake. Glacier outburst floods or *jökulhlaups* (see pages 122-123) can also turn into lahars if they mix with volcanic material.

A lahar is often quite small when it starts but quickly grows as it picks up snow, ice or running water along with loose rocks and vegetation. This added material can increase its volume by a factor of up to ten. As a lahar runs down the sides of a volcano and into surrounding valleys, it will typically keep going for tens of kilometres before it slows and eventually stops. In extreme cases, a lahar can flow for more than 100 km from its source volcano. Lahars tend to leave in their wake large deposits of sediment, up to several hundred metres thick, which can be enough to bury whole towns. Once laid down, the deposits tend to solidify quite rapidly, like fast-setting concrete, making escape difficult for anything or anyone trapped in them.

Most dangerous volcanoes

Scientists have identified a number of the world's volcanoes as the sources of particularly large lahars in the past and potential sources of future ones. The one considered most dangerous in this respect is Mount Rainier, a composite volcano in Washington State, USA, which last erupted in 1854. Large expanses of snow and ice – distributed in 26 glaciers – cover its summit and upper slopes; it also has a small crater lake.

About 5000 years ago, a massive lahar from Mount Rainier surged some 70 km across Washington State to reach the region on Puget Sound now occupied by the city of Tacoma and the southern suburbs of Seattle. It produced mud deposits 80 m deep in places and covered more than 320 km^2 of the north-western corner of the state. Other smaller lahars have flowed from Mount Rainier since then, and several towns in the area around the volcano, including parts of Tacoma, are built on old lahar deposits. It is possible that another lahar could be triggered of a comparable size to the event of 5000 years ago. If that happened, it would bury some of these towns, possibly destroy the centre of Seattle and cause tsunamis in Puget Sound.

To safeguard the population around Mount Rainier, a lahar warning system was set up in 1998. This consists of numerous seismometers placed around the volcano to detect tremors that might indicate the beginning of a lahar. Any positive signals are relayed to monitoring stations that immediately sound alarms, encouraging people to move to higher ground.

Mount Ruapehu, on New Zealand's North Island, poses a similar threat. Snow and glaciers blanket its slopes and, as on

ASH AND WATER After the 1991 eruption of Mount Pinatubo in the Philippines, a monsoon lashed the area, mixing rainwater and volcanic ash. The resulting lahars buried a vast region in mud and killed 1500 people.

BRIDGE OVER MUD In 2007, a bridge built to span the Whangaehu River in New Zealand's North Island became a route over a fast-moving lahar from Mount Ruapehu.

Mount Rainier, the summit contains a crater lake. Numerous medium-sized lahars have flowed from the volcano in the past, including one in 1953 that destroyed a railway bridge and caused New Zealand's worst-ever train disaster, with the loss of 151 lives. As with Mount Rainier, a lahar warning system has now been set up on Ruapehu. This was put to the test on March 18, 2007, when a dam holding back the volcano's crater lake burst, sending an estimated 1.4 million m³ of mud, rock and water thundering down the mountainside. The warning system worked, and there were no injuries or fatalities.

Indonesian lahars

The word 'lahar' is of Indonesian origin, reflecting the fact that the country has suffered many devastating lahars. The source of several of these has been Kelut, a composite volcano in eastern Java, mainly because of a crater lake at its summit. Records show that Kelut has erupted more than 30 times since AD 1000. In 1586, a series of deadly lahars swept down its slopes, destroying villages and killing 10 000 people. On May 19, 1919, another eruption killed 5110 people, destroyed about 9000 houses and submerged 135 km² of arable land. Lahars caused most of the devastation, travelling up to 39 km at an average speed of 25 km/h. Following this disaster, the authorities undertook an ambitious engineering project to drain the crater lake, and eruptions since then have been far less deadly, but Kelut is not Java's only source of lahars.

In 1822, pyroclastic flows and lahars from another composite volcano – Galunggung, at the western end of Java – killed more than 4000 people and destroyed 114 villages. Further devastating lahars followed an eruption in 1982. Since then, a crater lake has formed in the summit of Galunggung. This lake, combined with high rainfall in the area and large amounts of loose ash and other material on the volcano, has increased the risk of future lahars. Consequently, a warning system has been established.

Tragedy in Nicaragua

In October 1998, intense rainfall during Hurricane Mitch triggered a tragic lahar at the Casita volcano in Nicaragua, Central America. During the peak period of rainfall, a water-saturated flank of the volcano collapsed, starting off a lahar that killed more than 2000 people as it swept over the towns of Rolando Rodriguez and El Porvenir. Witnesses reported that the only warning of the lahar's approach was a noise sounding like thunder or helicopters, and a ground tremor that made some people think an earthquake was striking. Within three minutes, the lahar had overrun the towns, killing almost everybody. In this case, even if the flow had been detected by either instruments or an observer, the speed of the lahar and lack of nearby high ground would have prevented all but a few people from escaping.

THE MOST DEADLY SERIES OF LAHARS IN

RECORDED HISTORY FOLLOWED THE ERUPTION OF THE NEVADO DEL RUIZ VOLCANO IN COLOMBIA ON NOVEMBER 13, 1985. Over a period of a few hours, an estimated 23 000 people died as massive rivers of melted ice, mixed with volcanic ash and soil, surged down the sides of the volcano. Worst hit was the town of Armero, where 21 000 people were either swept away and drowned or asphyxiated by an 8 m thick wall of mud that submerged their homes in the dead of night.

The disaster began at 9.30 pm when an eruption from Nevado del Ruiz produced a series of pyroclastic flows. These were not particularly large, but a huge mass of ice covering the volcano's summit made them deadly. As the hot pyroclastic material settled on top of the icecap, about 10 per cent of the ice melted. This set off a series of small lahars that funnelled into six major river valleys. Heavy rain had also fallen recently, so they took in extra water as they descended. This increased their volume and momentum severalfold – in some canyons, the lahars were 50 m thick and flowed at 60 km/h.

Armero, some 70 km from Nevado del Ruiz's summit, lies a few kilometres downstream from where two of the lahars flowed into each other. Accounts from survivors indicate that several pulses of flowing material inundated the town. The first arrived 150 minutes after the original eruption and consisted of a flood of cold, relatively clean water – from a lake just upstream. The largest pulse arrived a few minutes later. Within 20 minutes, it had destroyed most of Armero.

A lack of preparation contributed to the high death toll. Armero had been built directly on old mudflows, and the authorities ignored a hazard-zone map showing the danger. When the eruption started, citizens were told to stay inside to avoid falling ash, with no mention of mudflows that could bury them. Today, a warning system is in place in the region.

MAXIMUM SPEED: 60 km/h
MAXIMUM DEPTH: 50 m
FARTHEST DISTANCE TRAVELLED:
    100 km
DEATHS CAUSED: 23 000
HOMES DESTROYED: 5000
ECONOMIC COST OF DISASTER:
    US $7.7 billion

WHITE DANGER

ONE OF THE 20TH CENTURY'S MOST EXTREME 'FREAKS OF NATURE' STRUCK THE SMALL SKIING RESORT OF GALTÜR IN THE AUSTRIAN TYROL ON FEBRUARY 23, 1999. It took the form of a gigantic wall of snow, up to 50 m high, which swept into the village without warning at a speed of some 200 km/h. Galtür had been isolated for several days before the avalanche struck – all roads into the village had been blocked by recent heavy snowfalls. Little skiing had been possible because of difficulties with ski lifts and the risk of avalanches. At about 4 pm on February 23, local inhabitants and holidaymakers were going about their business in the centre of the resort when the rushing white mass hit. Estimated to contain some 300 000 tonnes of snow, it overturned cars, destroyed seven buildings and buried more than 55 people. It was one of the largest, and certainly the deadliest, snow avalanche in the Alps in 40 years. Many of the victims died rapidly from inhaling and suffocating on the fluffy, low-density snow. Some people were dug out alive, but a total of 31 died.

Types of avalanche

A snow avalanche occurs when a massive chunk of snow breaks loose from a mountainside and shatters as it races downhill under the influence of gravity. All snow exists as layers with varying degrees of cohesiveness – the degree to which individual snowflakes stick to each other and to underlying snow layers. In general, snow avalanches happen when a weaker (less cohesive) layer of snow can no longer support the weight of the stronger (more cohesive) snow above it. Within that broad definition, experts recognise three main varieties of snow avalanche – wet avalanches, dry slab avalanches and powder avalanches.

Wet avalanches happen when the amount of liquid water within a mass of snow increases, usually as a result of rain or a rise in temperature, which causes partial melting. The presence of the liquid water makes the snow pack weaker and lubricates movement. Wet avalanches may start from a single point, spreading as they slide, or begin as a moving slab. They progress relatively slowly, at about 30–80 km/h, depending on their size.

MOVING SNOW Rescue teams begin the task of excavating buildings and retrieving bodies from the avalanche that engulfed the ski resort of Galtür in February 1999.

Dry slab avalanches occur at below freezing temperatures when a slope becomes overloaded with snow. This is usually a result of heavy snowfalls combined with wind, which pile up the snow in particular areas. The avalanche starts as a cohesive chunk of dry snow, which breaks free as a unit and then fractures as it slides. Once started, it typically accelerates within a few seconds to downhill speeds of 40–150 km/h, depending on size.

Powder avalanches generally start from a single point and grow as they progress. Ever-increasing masses of powder snow are thrown into the air, flowing down the slope as a dense cloud. The largest avalanches may reach speeds of 300 km/h, and the shock waves that precede them can flatten everything in their path. Although rare, this type is extremely dangerous – a powder avalanche caused the 1999 Galtür disaster.

Trigger factors

Many different factors affect the likelihood that an avalanche will occur. Most happen on slopes angled between 35 and 45 degrees. Slopes shallower than 30 degrees are usually too stable for an avalanche to develop; on slopes steeper than 50 degrees, small slides of fresh powder snow happen so often that the snow never builds up in sufficient quantity for an avalanche. Terrain is also important – avalanches are always more likely to occur on treeless slopes and where the surface underlying the snow consists of relatively smooth grass or slabs of rock.

Other key factors are weather-related and act together. The most important is a high rate of snowfall within the preceding 24–48 hours – the risk of an avalanche is nearly always high after a storm that has deposited 300 mm or more of fresh snow. Wind speed and direction are also important, as the wind can redistribute the snow, piling it up in some areas of a slope to form an unstable mass.

Equally important is the type of snow within each layer in the snowpack. For an avalanche to happen, at least one weak layer of snow – a layer that is not strongly bound to the underlying layer – must be present. Above this weak layer lie more strongly bound layers. This means that avalanche risk is influenced by the whole history of the types of snow that have fallen in an area over several weeks.

Other factors include changes in temperature and the amount of solar radiation. A sudden rise in temperature, causing snow to melt, can trigger a wet avalanche. A period of thaw, followed by later freezing, can create a hard crust of snow that a subsequent snow layer will have difficulty adhering to. This will set up potential avalanche conditions some days or even weeks into the future.

Once the conditions are ripe, it is frequently people – skiers, snowboarders or snowmobilers – who provide the final trigger factor by adding further excess weight to a mass of snow that has already become unstable.

Analysing Galtür

Avalanche experts spent several years analysing the 1999 Galtür disaster, anxious to learn from it all that they could. Until then, the centre of the village had been considered almost completely safe from avalanche risk. What they found was that the Galtür avalanche was the result of a highly unusual combination of weather-related factors that are unlikely to be repeated more than once every few hundred years. These included three weather systems originating from the Atlantic that caused record snowfalls in the Alps over the preceding week. At the same time, high winds and low temperatures meant that exceptionally large volumes of snow accumulated quickly in certain locations.

In the Galtür area, these large accumulations formed on top of a weak snow layer, created about a week before the disaster by a quick thaw followed by a freeze. When this weak layer failed and a relatively small powder avalanche began, conditions on the surface were ripe for the initial slide of powder snow to set off snow layers lower down the slope that were close to their threshold for movement. In this way, the avalanche picked up more than double the amount of the initial volume of snow as it travelled down the mountain. Finally, the steep alpine landscape intensified the effect of the avalanche.

Predicting and preventing

Nowadays, great efforts are made to minimise avalanche risks in ski resorts. These rely on a combination of day-to-day monitoring of weather and snow conditions – especially the characteristics of the different layers of snow – and the historical record of avalanches in particular areas. Preventative measures include the use of computer simulations, based on worst-case scenarios for the amount of snow that an avalanche might theoretically contain, to calculate hazard zones within resorts: those at highest risk of an avalanche and those with a low or negligible risk. Buildings and facilities such as ski lifts are located in low-risk zones.

Other precautions include the construction of anti-avalanche barriers (snow fences) on vulnerable slopes and the setting off of explosive charges after heavy snowfalls. The latter helps to bring down any dangerous accumulations of snow in a controlled way. A third method concentrates on warning and educating people about the risks and triggering factors for avalanches. In Europe, for example, coloured flags are displayed on slopes to warn skiers and other recreationists of the risk level.

Despite these measures, accidents do happen as a result of avalanches. The victims are usually people who have gone 'off piste' – strayed away, intentionally or accidentally, from maintained and monitored areas – and set off an avalanche themselves. In most cases, the avalanche is a dry slab one. Victims find themselves on or below the moving slab, with little chance of escaping as it breaks up and carries them down the slope.

CHANCES OF SURVIVAL

The time it takes to dig avalanche victims out of the snow plays a large part in deciding whether or not they will survive. Even the densest snow contains trapped air, so when someone is buried, there is no initial problem in breathing, but the carbon dioxide the person breathes out quickly builds up, displaces the oxygen and causes gradual suffocation. If dug out within five minutes, someone has about a 90 per cent chance of still being alive, but after 45 minutes only about 20–30 per cent of victims are still alive.

Skiers, climbers and others who put themselves at risk of avalanches are advised to carry a kit containing an avalanche transceiver (a device that sends out an electronic signal when buried in snow and can also be used to locate the position of another transceiver), together with a collapsible metal probe and a shovel, which can help to locate and dig out buried victims. It may take half an hour or more to summon professional rescuers, so the chances of avalanche victims surviving often depend heavily on the ability of other members of their party to rescue them.

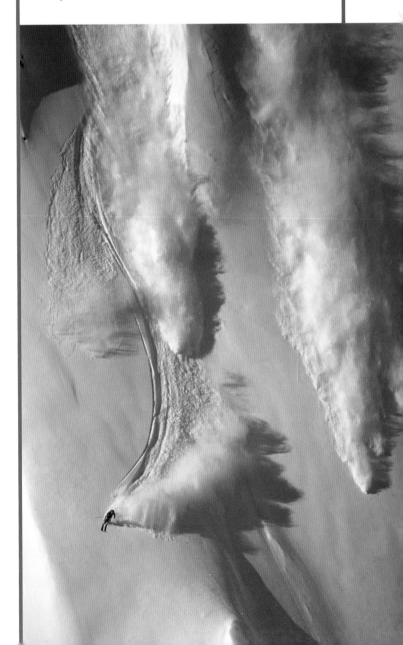

PLUMMETING ICE

EVEN MORE TERRIFYING THAN A SNOW AVALANCHE IS ONE CONSISTING OF MASSIVE, HARD, ANGULAR CHUNKS OF ICE. In general, ice avalanches occur when a large mass of ice breaks off from the end of a steep mountain glacier or from any overhanging part of it.

The ice then slides down the mountainside, breaking up as it goes. Because most glaciers contain appreciable amounts of rock – which has either been wrenched off mountainsides by the glacier or fallen onto and been absorbed by the glacier – so do ice avalanches. Experts have not yet discovered any specific triggering factors for mountainside ice avalanches. They can occur at any time of day, in any season and in a variety of weather conditions. In short, they are highly unpredictable.

A more predictable type of ice avalanche occurs at sea level, when chunks of ice break off from the snouts of glaciers that have reached the ocean, fall into the water and float away as icebergs. Iceberg calving, as this is known, is so spectacular it has become a popular tourist attraction in places such as the fjords of Alaska and southern Chile and around the islands of Svalbard in the Arctic Ocean.

The ice fell 900 m into a gorge, and shortly afterwards, a 125 m wall of ice fragments burst out of the gorge at its lower end, hurtling down the mountain at a speed of more than 160 km/h. Tearing dirt, rock and boulders from the slopes, the ice travelled 16 km.

Areas of risk

Terrifying though they can be, most mountain ice avalanches do not pose any great risk to people, because they occur in areas with low population density – remote regions of Alaska and western China, for example. But some happen in more populated areas or ones that are visited by large numbers of tourists, such as the Swiss Alps, where the unpredictability and sheer destructive power can lead to a major human disaster.

The deadliest in recorded history struck in the Peruvian Andes on January 10, 1962, when a chunk of ice weighing several million tonnes broke loose from a 50 m thick icecap on the north summit of the 7000 m peak, Huascarán (eight years later, the same mountain unleashed one of the deadliest recorded landslides, see page 130). The ice fell 900 m into a gorge, and shortly afterwards, a 125 m wall of ice fragments burst out of the gorge at its lower end, hurtling down the mountain at a speed of more than 160 km/h. Tearing dirt, rock and boulders from the slopes, the ice travelled 16 km and overwhelmed several communities, including the town of Ranrahirca. It killed about 4000 people and left a blanket of ice and rock debris, nearly 2 km wide and 13 m deep.

Three years later, on the afternoon of August 30, 1965, engineers and workers building a dam near Saas Fee in south-western Switzerland, near the border with Italy, suddenly heard a dull boom from the sky. The construction

site lay at the foot of a sheer rock wall above the Saas valley. Sitting just on top of the wall was the lower end of the 9 km long Allalin Glacier. Glancing up, the men saw a large chunk of the glacier break off and start sliding down the cliff, slowly at first and then in a quickening whirl of ice and rock. One eyewitness reported, 'A giant wind blew me down. I kept crawling on my hands and knees. I was engulfed by ice; it covered me to my chin.' Within 20 seconds, the whole work site lay buried beneath a blanket of ice, 30 m deep. Twelve people died.

In June 1981, 11 mountain climbers died in similar circumstances as they ascended Mount Rainier in Washington State, USA. A wall of ice suddenly broke off the face of one the mountain's large glaciers and buried the climbers under 20 m of ice and other debris. In Switzerland's Bernese Oberland, there have also been avalanches, involving up to 300 000 m³ of ice, from hanging glaciers on the south flank of the 4099 m peak, the Mönch – a neighbour of the more famous Eiger and Jungfrau. The run-out zones of these ice falls have sometimes spewed across a popular walking route from the nearby Jungfraujoch, but so far there have been no accidents.

CALVING GLACIER A massive block of ice detaches itself from the 80 m high calving face of Alaska's Hubbard Glacier and plunges into the ocean.

FORCES AND ENE

RGY

7

VOLCANIC ERUPTIONS, GUSHING GEYSERS, EARTHQUAKES, LIGHTNING STRIKES, LANDSLIDES – MANY DRAMATIC NATURAL phenomena are forms of energy transformation taking place within the Earth's crust or on its surface. To understand the original sources of this energy, it is necessary to delve into the fundamental forces of Nature that underlie everything in the Universe. These forces are involved in every process on the planet, from the accumulation of heat and chemical energy in Earth's interior, to gas explosions, to the ebb and flow of tides, to the extraordinary pushes and pulls that drive tectonic plate movements. Believed by physicists to have originated in the Big Bang, these fundamental forces have influenced Earth throughout its 4.6 billion year history and they continue to be at the centre of all observable natural phenomena.

GRAVITY

ATTRACTION BETWEEN OBJECTS Gravity is the attractive force between objects. Uniquely among the four forces, gravity acts between all objects and at all distances. It is the dominant force on a planetary scale – for example, causing objects to fall to the ground – and on all larger scales, holding stars and galaxies together. On Earth, gravity plays a part in processes such as tectonic plate movement and tides.

HOLDING ATOMS TOGETHER The strong nuclear force attracts protons and neutrons together within the nuclei of atoms. It is the strongest of the four forces, but it is not quite powerful enough to keep some large atomic nuclei intact forever. Some nuclei partially break up, in a process called alpha radioactive decay, with the release of a tiny amount of heat energy. Because of this, radioactive materials generate heat.

STRONG NUCLEAR

FUNDAMENTAL FORCES

PHYSICAL PHENOMENA IN THE UNIVERSE, ...UDING ALL TYPES OF ENERGY RELEASE ON ...TH, CAN BE EXPLAINED BY FOUR FUNDAMENTAL ...CES – gravity, the electromagnetic force, the ...ng nuclear force and the weak nuclear force.

...orce describes a different way in which the objects and particles ...make up the world interact with each other. Gravity is the force that ...objects towards each other. The larger the objects, the stronger ...traction. The electromagnetic force only operates between matter ...ticles carrying an electric charge, and causes electrical and ...etic effects. The strong and weak nuclear forces operate within the ...of atoms, holding them together, and govern radioactive decay. The ...are described as 'fundamental' because each is distinct and cannot ...plained in terms of other, more basic interactions.

Physicists have looked for links between the forces, to see if they ...built into a unifying model to describe the whole Universe, a ...led 'Theory of Everything'. For three of the forces – the strong and ...nuclear forces and the electromagnetic force – messenger particles ...gauge bosons have been discovered that play key roles in the ...tion of the forces. It is suggested, though not proven, that just after ...ig Bang, these three forces were unified in a single force, and that as

temperatures dropped over time the forces separated out – the strong nuclear force first, followed by a splitting of the weak nuclear and electromagnetic forces. There is further speculation that a fraction of a second earlier, all four forces were unified in a single force, and that as the temperature dropped, they separated – gravity first, followed by the other three. A model of the Universe that links all the forces in this way is called the Grand Unified Theory.

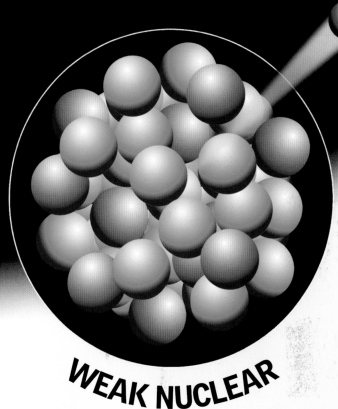

WEAK NUCLEAR

ACTIVE WITHIN ATOMS Like the strong nuclear force, the weak nuclear force operates over tiny distances, less than the diameter of the nucleus of an atom. It plays a part in beta radioactive decay – a type of alteration in the structure of an atomic nucleus. Beta decay is most commonly accompanied by the emission of an electron together with a tiny amount of energy.

ELECTROMAGNETIC

ATTRACTION AND REPULSION The electromagnetic force acts between electrically charged particles, attracting particles with different charges (one positive, one negative) and repelling particles with the same charge. It is the second-strongest force after the strong nuclear force. It plays a part in the generation of light and radiant heat, and controls the storage of chemical energy.

EARTH'S ENERGY AND GRAVITY

PULLING POWER The power of the mutual gravitational attraction between the Earth and the Moon can be seen in the ebb and flow of the tides.

SOME 4.57 BILLION YEARS AGO, GRAVITY BROUGHT ABOUT THE EARTH'S FORMATION, JUST AS IT WAS RESPONSIBLE FOR FORMING THE SUN AND THE OTHER PLANETS. It was also responsible for the Earth being born in a hot, molten state, and it helped determine our planet's basic structure of core, mantle and crust. Gravity still plays a part in driving the tectonic plate movements that give rise to volcanic eruptions and earthquakes, and in many types of energy-transforming processes at Earth's surface, including tides, rainfall, erosion and landslides.

Gravitational potential energy

Crucial to understanding gravity's role in the early history of our planet is the concept of gravitational potential energy. This is the energy that objects possess by virtue of their position relative to other objects.

Imagine two objects located in space some 500 m apart. Each object possesses some energy – gravitational potential energy – because of the gravitational pull exerted on it by the other object. As a result of their mutual attraction (and in the absence of any other forces), the two objects accelerate towards each other. As their speed increases and they approach each other, their potential energy is converted into energy of movement, or kinetic energy. When the objects eventually collide, the kinetic energy is converted into other forms of energy, notably heat energy.

During Earth's formation a similar process occurred, but on a grander scale. Countless billions of tiny particles of dust and gas, within a vast cloud of such material, gradually accreted through the effects of gravity until eventually they formed a single, compact body. As this happened, the gravitational potential energy of the original cloud of material was converted into heat, and our planet started life in a hot, molten state.

Gravity's work was not finished with Earth's formation. In the early Earth, heavy elements sank towards the centre and lighter elements migrated towards the surface, starting the process by which Earth's interior became differentiated into a core, mantle and crust. As this led to a further concentration of mass towards Earth's centre, more gravitational energy was released as heat. There is some evidence that this gravitational sorting is still going on, billions of years after Earth was first formed, and continues to warm the planet's interior.

Gravity contributes to tectonic-plate movements, and to the events that follow on from them, because through its action of causing less dense material (for example, heated mantle rocks in the lower mantle) to rise towards Earth's surface, and denser material (cooler rocks in the upper mantle) to sink, it is partly responsible for the convective flow of heat energy in Earth's mantle.

NUCLEAR
FORCES

ALPHA DECAY *ALPHA DECAY Some radioactive materials, such as pellets of plutonium-238, produce heat energy at such a rate that they glow in the dark.*

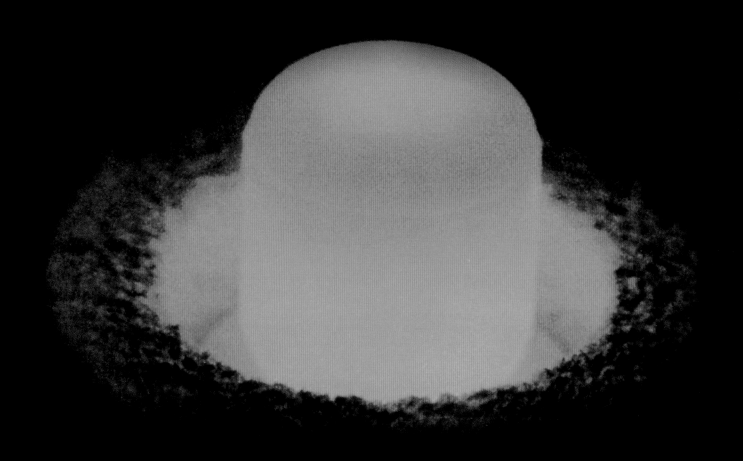

The decay of uranium-238 generates heat within Earth's crust at a rate of about a trillion joules per second, or one terawatt.

THE NUCLEI OF ALL ATOMS ARE MADE OF PROTONS (POSITIVELY CHARGED PARTICLES) AND NEUTRONS (UNCHARGED PARTICLES). These particles are bound together by a powerful force called the strong nuclear force. However, some atomic nuclei are not completely stable. In these nuclei, the strong nuclear force cannot keep all the protons and neutrons bound together forever, as there is an opposing tendency for the protons to repel each other and break up the nucleus. In the process known as radioactive decay, unstable nuclei undergo partial disintegration, ejecting part of themselves. Whenever one of these spontaneous disintegrations occurs, it produces a little heat – and it is this heat, generated by trillions of nuclei disintegrations, that helps to drive many natural phenomena, such as earthquakes and volcanic eruptions.

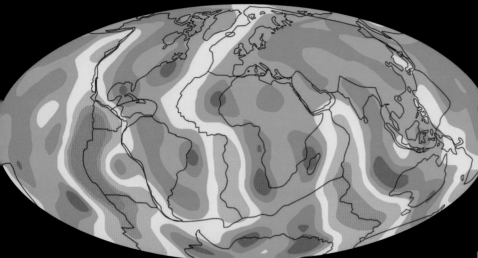

HEAT TRANSFER FROM EARTH'S INTERIOR The map shows variations in the rate at which Earth's internal heat – which is partly generated by radioactive decay – flows out at the planet's surface. The highest flow rates (red, orange and yellow) tend to be along mid-ocean ridges.

0   40   60   80   100   120   240   350

Kilowatts per km²

One substance whose atoms undergo radioactive decay is uranium. In Earth's crust, uranium is mainly present as the isotope uranium-238 (an isotope is a particular form of a chemical element). The nucleus of uranium-238 is only slightly unstable, but in any large collection, disintegrations of the type known as alpha decay occur regularly. In each decay an alpha particle, which consists of two protons and two neutrons, is ejected at high speed from the nucleus.

Heat generation

When an alpha decay occurs, a small amount of mass is converted into kinetic energy as the products of the decay rush away from each other. This released energy ultimately causes a slight heating of the rock where the alpha decay happened. It is possible to measure the amount of energy released in each alpha decay: in a uranium-238 nucleus, it is about one-trillionth of a joule. This might seem negligible, but within a single gram of uranium, more than 12 000 alpha decays occur every second. As the amount of uranium-238 contained in Earth's crust is about 100 000 trillion kg, the decay of uranium-238 generates heat within Earth's crust at a rate of about a trillion joules per second, or one terawatt. Thorium-232 also produces about a terawatt of energy, and uranium-235 chips in another fraction of a terawatt. Many of the decay products of these substances also undergo alpha decays, generating yet more heat. All these substances are also present in Earth's mantle, where again they generate considerable heat.

Some unstable atomic nuclei undergo other types of radioactive decay, most commonly one called beta decay. There are different types of beta decay, and they are an effect of the weak nuclear force. In beta decay, instead of emitting alpha particles, atomic nuclei emit or absorb electrons, or emit positrons (antielectrons).

An important radioactive isotope in Earth's crust that undergoes beta decay is potassium-40. The amount of energy released by a beta decay is less than that from an alpha decay,

but there are many thousands of trillions of tonnes of potassium-40 in Earth's crust and mantle, and each gram of potassium-40 undergoes about 230 000 beta decays per second, so this adds up to several more terawatts of heat output. Potassium-40 may also be present in Earth's core, where its radioactive breakdown releases heat at an estimated rate of half a terawatt.

Recent studies indicate that the total heat generation by radioactivity is about 24 terawatts. This accounts for about two-thirds of the total rate at which heat energy is currently being generated within, and flowing out from, our planet.

BETA DECAY In the most common variety of beta decay, an electron is released from a nucleus together with a little energy.

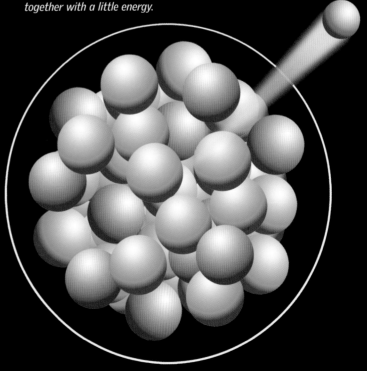

ELECTROMAGNETIC FORCE

THE ELECTROMAGNETIC (EM) FORCE PLAYS A PART IN ALMOST ALL ASPECTS OF EVERYDAY EXISTENCE, from the workings of technical inventions such as mobile phones and microwave ovens, to natural phenomena such as friction, rainbows and lightning. It controls chemical reactions and the storage of chemical energy in different substances; and it plays a part in the generation of light and radiant heat. Although it has an infinite range, in practice most of its main effects are exerted over very short distances.

Chemical energy

The EM force holds the atoms within a nucleus together by attracting the negatively charged electrons, which move around in the outer parts of each atom, to the positively charged protons that reside in the atomic nuclei. Without the EM force, the electrons would simply fly off. And the EM force holds molecules together by controlling the formation of bonds between the molecule's constituent atoms. In each case, there is some sharing or transfer of electrons between the participating atoms.

In chemical reactions, bonds between molecules are broken or formed. Some reactions are energy-consuming, while other reactions are energy-releasing. A substance described as a store of chemical energy has a high potential to take part in energy-releasing reactions – by decomposition or by reaction with a commonly available substance, such as oxygen.

In Earth's crust, the main stores of chemical energy are fossil fuels. This energy can be released by a reaction between the fossil fuels and oxygen to form carbon dioxide and water. Most of this energy release occurs in a controlled way in human-invented devices, such as the internal combustion engine. But explosive releases of chemical energy sometimes occur spontaneously or by accident – as in gas and coaldust explosions in coalmines, or explosions at oil storage facilities.

Lightning energy

One of the most obvious types of explosive energy release involving the EM force is lightning. In a lightning strike, a sudden movement of electrical charges occurs between a cloud and the ground following a separation of positive and negative charges within the cloud. Each lightning strike generates about a billion joules of energy, which would be enough to power a 100-watt lightbulb continuously for about four months.

ENERGY RELEASE Fossil fuels such as oil and gas are a store of chemical energy within the Earth's crust. The potency of this energy store was illustrated by an explosion in 2005 at the Buncefield oil storage depot in Hertfordshire, England.

ELECTROMAGNETIC LIGHTSHOW The aurora borealis, or northern lights, is caused by electrically charged particles from the Sun colliding with atoms in Earth's atmosphere. The atoms become energised, and release energy as light.

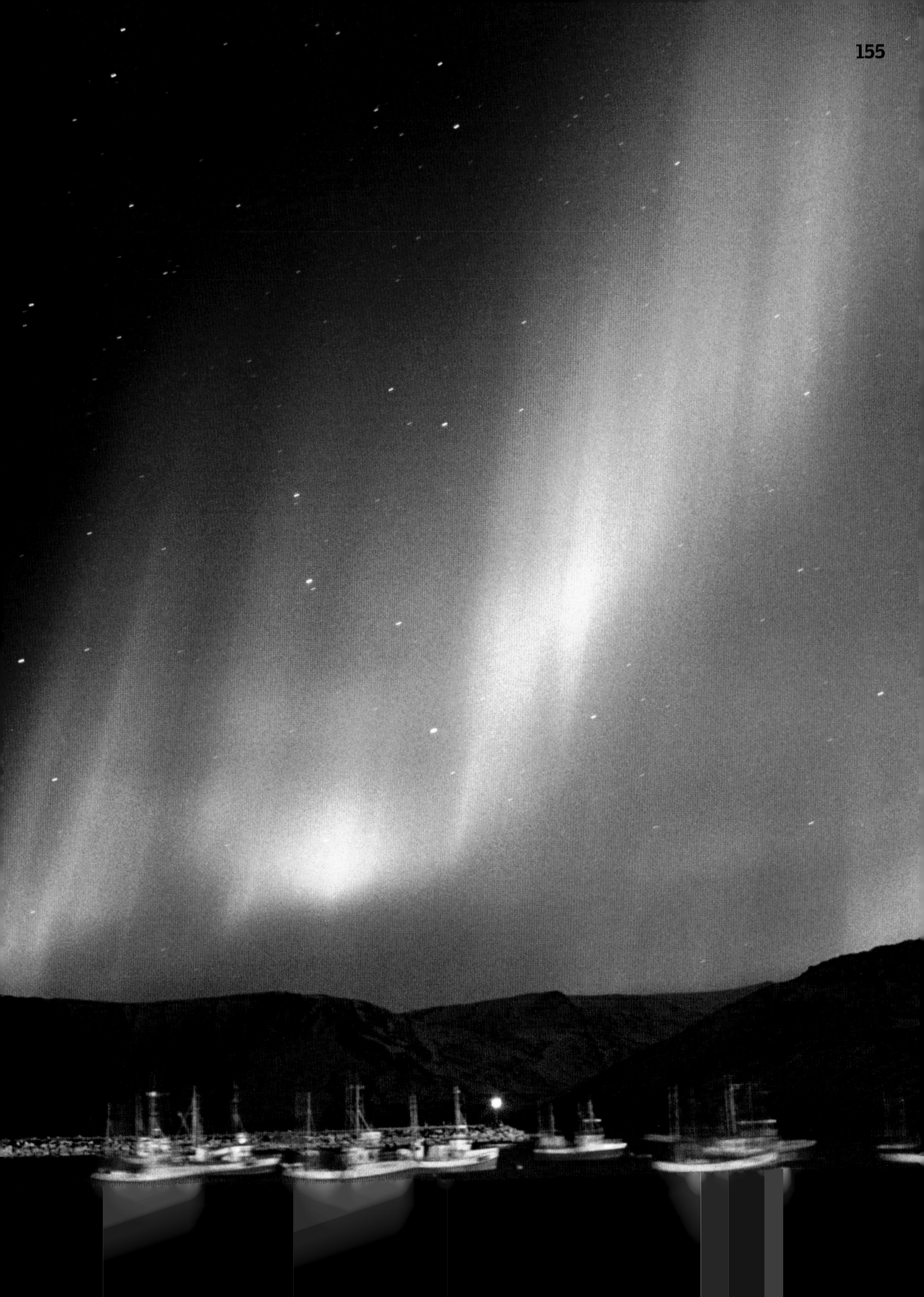

INDEX

A

Africa 13, 21, 25, 28, 32, 34, 35, 82, 83, 118–119, 135
African Plate 21, 24, 25, 51
Alaska 30, 38, 55, 81, 144–145
Aleppo (Syria) 51
Aleutian Islands 30, 31, 55, 103
Algeria 52, 53
Algiers 53
Alps 28, 123, 128–129, 140–141, 143, 144
ammonia 79
Anak Krakatau (Indonesia) 103
Anatolian Plate 40
Andaman Islands 6
Andes 23, 27, 92, 123, 124, 130, 144
Antarctic Plate 20–21
Antarctica 34, 35, 78–79
Antigua 93
Arabian Plate 20, 21, 25, 40
Arctic 121
Arctic Ocean 144
Ardabil (Iran) 51
Argentina 124
Armero (Colombia) 92, 139
arsenic sulphide 112
Asaka Pagoda 58
ash, volcanic 3, 16, 18, 61–63, 67, 68, 71–73, 77–81, 83–88, 90–93, 95, 102–107, 122, 129, 135–139
Ashgabat (Turkmenistan) 51
Asia 28, 34, 51, 117, 123
Atlantic Ocean 51, 96, 99, 100–101, 104, 105, 135, 143
  Mid-Atlantic Ridge 21, 24, 29
Australasian Plate 21, 27, 31, 103, 107
Australia 34, 35, 117
Austria 4, 140–141
avalanches 51, 123, 128–130, 134, 138, 140–145
  Galtür (Austria) 4, 12, 140–143
  Hispar Peak (Pakistan) 142
  Huascarán (Peru) 130
  predicting and preventing 143
  see also ice falls; lahars; landslides; mudflows
Awaji island (Japan) 32, 49
Azerbaijan 116–117

B

Balakot (Kashmir) 52
Bali 71, 103
Bam (Iran) 39, 52–53
Banda Aceh (Sumatra) 39
basalt 20, 67, 71, 75, 77, 99
Batang Lupar bore 127
Bernese Oberland 145
Bhachau (India) 51
Bhutan 123

Big Bang 147, 149
Black Rock Desert (Nevada) 109
Bocca Grande (Italy) 112
Bogoslof Island (Aleutians) 103
bores, tidal 126–127
Borneo 88
Brazo Rico Lake (Argentina) 124
Brimstone Pit (Mariana Islands) 103
Buncefield oil storage depot 154
Burma Plate 54

C

calderas 3, 67, 68, 85, 91, 122
California 19, 20, 29, 40, 43, 44–45, 51, 64, 132, 135
Cameroon 118–119
Canary Islands 65, 96, 99, 135
cap rock 19
Cape Verde Islands 99
carbon dioxide 13, 79, 91, 112, 116, 118–119, 121, 143, 154
Caribbean 3, 71, 80, 87, 93, 100–102
Caribbean Plate 20, 31, 101
Central America 138
Chagos Islands 99
Channeled Scablands (USA) 123
Chi-Chi earthquake 30, 47
Chile 31, 38, 55, 110, 114, 144
China 4, 6, 50–52, 56–57, 121, 127, 144
Chuandongbei gas field (China) 120–121
cinders, volcanic 67, 68, 72, 77–79, 88, 104, 105, 107
cliffs, collapse of 130–131, 134
climate change 5, 18, 84, 85, 88, 91, 121
coalmines 6, 13, 120, 121, 154
Cocos Plate 20, 31, 52
Colombia 64, 79, 88, 92, 139
Colorado 85
Columbia Plateau (USA) 71
Congo, Democratic Republic of 65, 70, 76, 89
continental drift 34, 35
Cordillera Blanca (Peru) 123
core (Earth's) 17, 18, 42, 96, 151, 153
Costa Rica 31, 68
Crater Lake (Oregon) 68
craters, volcanic 63, 67, 68, 74–77, 82, 83, 89, 99, 102, 112, 119
  crater lakes see under lakes
creep (soil movement) 131
Crete 91
crust (Earth's) 15, 17, 18, 20, 22–25, 27, 28, 32, 37, 38, 54, 63, 64, 66, 82, 96, 101, 110, 117, 147, 151–154

D

Damghan (Iran) 51
Darwin, Charles 98
Dead Sea 24

Deccan Traps (India) 99
deserts 132, 135
Dominica 100, 101
Dordogne, River 127

E

Earth 127, 147, 148, 150
  formation of 16–18, 151
  temperature of 16–18
  see also core; crust; mantle
earthquakes 15, 18, 22, 25, 27–32, 36–59, 73, 86, 91–93, 102, 109, 115, 123, 130, 132, 134, 137, 147, 151, 152
  aftermath of 43, 47, 48
  aftershocks 48, 54
  Alaska 30, 38
  Aleutian Islands 30
  Aleppo (Syria) 51
  Algeria 52, 53
  Ardabil (Iran) 51
  Ashgabat (Turkmenistan) 51
  Bam (Iran) 39, 52–53
  Bandah Aceh (Sumatra) 39
  building collapse 38, 39, 40–41, 43, 44, 46–47, 50, 51, 52–53
  causes of 38–41
  Chi-Chi 30, 47
  Chile 31, 38, 55
  control of 57
  Damghan (Iran) 51
  deadliest 50–53
  detecting and measuring 42–43
  Ecuador 31
  Fiji 30
  firestorms 12, 37, 47, 50, 51
  Guatemala 31
  Gujarat (India) 39, 50–51
  Haicheng (China) 57
  Hebgen Lake (Montana) 115
  Helike (Greece) 50, 51
  Indian Ocean (2004) 6, 27, 51, 54–55
  infrastructure damage 36–37, 44–45, 48, 49
  Izmit (Turkey) 39, 40–41
  Java 30
  Kamchatka (Russia) 30
  Kanto (Japan) 30, 39, 51
  Kashmir 39, 52, 53
  Kermadec Islands 30
  Kobe (Japan) 12, 30–32, 39, 47, 49
  Kuril Islands 30
  Lisbon 51
  Los Angeles 31, 44
  magnitude of 42–43, 57
  Messina (Sicily) 39, 51
  Mexico City 31, 38, 48, 52, 53
  Middle East 51
  Niagata (Japan) 30
  Ningxia-Gansu (China) 51
  Oakland (California) 44–45
  Papua New Guinea 30
  Peru 31, 38
  Philippines 30

  predictions of (in China) 56–57
  quake-proofing 56–59
  in 'Ring of Fire' 30–31
  San Francisco 29, 36–38, 47, 48, 51
  Shaanxi (China) 51
  Solomon Islands 30, 31, 39
  Spitak (Armenia) 39
  submarine 6, 54–55, 135
  Sumatra 4, 6, 30, 51
  Taipei 46-7
  Tangshan (China) 39, 51, 52, 56
  Tsinghai (China) 51
  see also plates, tectonic; tsunamis
East Africa 25, 82, 83
Ecuador 31, 62
Eiger 145
El Porvenir (Nicaragua) 138
El Salvador 4, 5, 58, 132–133
electricity generation 18, 19
electromagnetic energy see under energy (Earth's)
Emperor Seamounts (Hawaii) 96
energy (Earth's) 109, 146–155
  electromagnetic 13, 149, 154–155
  geothermal 18, 19, 31, 85, 109, 110, 115
  gravity 13, 16, 17, 127, 129, 130, 140, 148–151
  hydrothermal 109, 110, 113, 115, 116
  kinetic 17, 151, 153
  lightning 146–147, 154
  nuclear 13, 148, 149, 152–153
  tidal 19, 126–127, 148, 150–151
  wind 19, 132, 142, 143
England 127, 154
Eritrea 25, 82
erosion 64, 98, 99, 105–107, 132, 134, 135, 151
Erta Ale (Ethiopia) 17, 67, 82, 83
eruptions, volcanic see volcanic eruptions
Española Island (Galápagos) 98
Ethiopia 17, 67, 82, 83
Eurasian Plate 20, 21, 23, 27, 28, 31, 40, 51, 53, 85, 103
Europe 28, 34, 127, 135, 143
evolution 34–35
extinction 121

F

Falcon Island (Tonga) 106
faults (geological) 15, 20, 21, 28, 29, 32, 38, 40, 51, 54, 57, 58, 117
Ferdinandea (Mediterranean) 105, 106
Fernandina Island (Galápagos) 96–98
Fernando de Noronha 99
Fiji 30
Fire Island (Aleutians) 103
firedamp 121

firestorms 12, 37, 47, 50, 51
Flores (Indonesia) 103
fossil fuels 120, 154
fossils 32, 34, 35
fumaroles 109, 110, 112

G

Gabustan Reserve (Azerbaijan)
    116–117
Galápagos Islands 94–99
Galápagos Spreading Centre 99
Galeras (Colombia) 31, 64, 79
Galtür (Austria) 4, 12, 140–143
Galunggung (Indonesia) 88, 138
Garonne, River 127
gas 3, 16, 27, 57, 61–63, 66–68,
    71–73, 78–81, 91, 92, 109, 112,
    113, 116, 117, 120–121, 151, 154
    gas explosions 6, 13, 118–121,
        147, 154
geothermal energy *see under*
    energy (Earth's)
geyserite 114, 115
geysers 13, 109, 110–111, 114–115,
    147
    Castle Geyser (Yellowstone) 114
    cone geysers 114–115
    El Tatio geyser field (Chile) 114
    Fly Geyser (Nevada) 108–109
    fountain geysers 114
    Geysers, The (California) 19
    Old Faithful (Yellowstone) 114
    Pohutu Geyser (NZ) 110–111
    Porkchop Geyser (Yellowstone)
        115
    Prince of Wales Feathers Geyser
        (NZ) 110–111
    Strokkur Geyser (Iceland)
        114–115
    Taupo volcanic zone (NZ) 114
    see also hot springs
Gironde bore 127
glaciers 64, 123, 130, 135, 137,
    144–145
    Allalin Glacier (Switzerland) 145
    Belvedere Glacier (Italy) 123
    Hubbard Glacier (Alaska)
        144–145
    Medvezhi Glacier (Tajikistan)
        123
    outburst floods 3, 13, 122–125,
        137
    Perito Merino Glacier
        (Argentina) 124
    Trakarding Glacier (Nepal) 125
Global Positioning System (GPS)
    32
global warming 121, 123
Glossopteris 35
Goma (DRC) 89
Gondwana 34
Grand Unified Theory 149
granite 20, 132
gravity *see under* energy (Earth's)
Great Rift Valley 24, 25, 82, 83
Greece 50, 65

greenhouse gases 18, 120, 121
Grenada 100–102
Guadeloupe 100, 101
Guatemala 31, 64
Gujarat (India) 39, 50–51
Gulf of Aqaba 24, 25
Gulf of Corinth 50

H

Hangzhou (China) 127
Hanshin (Japan) 30, 49
Har Megiddo 50
Hawaii 18, 23, 32, 55, 64, 67,
    69–71, 74–76, 96, 98, 99, 135
Heimaey (Iceland) 79
Helike (Greece) 51
Herculaneum 70, 88
High Atlas mountains 28
Himalayas 28, 123
Hispar Peak (Pakistan) 142
Holocene period 64
homelessness 49, 53, 89
Hong Kong 132
Honshu island (Japan) 30, 49, 106
Horn of Africa 25
hot springs 13, 18, 109–115
    Bajawa (Indonesia) 110
    Beppu (Japan) 112
    Deildartunguhver (Iceland) 110
    Mammoth Hot Springs (USA)
        112
    Solfatara (Italy) 112
    Wai-o-tapu (NZ) 112, 113
    Yudanka (Japan) 112
    see also geysers
hotspots 18, 23, 32, 64, 66, 85,
    96–99, 104, 105, 110, 135
Huaráz (Peru) 123
Huascarán (Peru) 130, 135, 144
Hurricane Mitch 3, 138
hydrocarbons 116
hydrogen 120
hydrogen chloride 79
hydrogen fluoride 79
hydrogen sulphide 79, 112, 113
hydrothermal chimneys 98
hydrothermal energy *see under*
    energy (Earth's)

I

ice 86, 92, 124–125, 129, 130, 135,
    137, 139, 144
ice falls 144–145
    Allalin Glacier (Switzerland) 145
    Huascarán (Peru) 144
    Mount Rainier (USA) 145
icebergs 124, 144
icecaps 3, 122, 123
Iceland 3, 4, 15, 18, 21, 70, 71, 79,
    88, 91, 104–105, 110, 114–115,
    122–123
India 6, 28, 34, 35, 51, 53, 85, 99
Indian Ocean 4–6, 12, 24, 27, 51,
    54–55, 85, 99, 103
Indian Plate 21, 28, 53, 54, 85, 99

Indonesia 4, 6, 18, 27, 39, 65, 71,
    85, 88, 103, 110, 117, 138
Iran 51, 53
iron 17, 114
Isabela Island (Galápagos) 94–97
islands, volcanic *see* volcanic
    islands
Israel 24
Istanbul 40
Italy 4, 5, 18, 65, 70, 72, 110, 112,
    123
Izmit (Turkey) 39, 40–41
Izu Island (Japan) 103

J

Japan 12, 18, 22, 23, 27, 30–32,
    39, 49, 51, 55–58, 65, 72, 88,
    103, 106, 110, 112
Java 30, 88, 103, 117, 138
jökulhlaups 3, 13, 122, 123, 125,
    137
Jordan 24, 25
Juan de Fuca Plate 20, 31
Juan Fernández Islands 99
Jungfrau 145
Jungfraujoch 145

K

Kagoshima (Japan) 65
Kamchatka (Russia) 26, 30, 31, 72
Kanto (Japan) 51
Kashmir 39, 52, 53
Kauai island (Hawaii) 98
Kelut (Indonesia) 88
Kermadec Islands 30
Kilauea (Hawaii) 69, 71, 75, 96, 98
kinetic energy *see under* energy
    (Earth's)
Kobe (Japan) 12, 30–32, 39, 47, 49
Krakatau (Indonesia) 71, 88
Kure atoll (Hawaii) 96
Kuril Islands 22, 23, 30, 31, 103
Kyoto 58

L

La Palma 135
Laccadive Islands 99
Laguna Beach 132
lahars 3, 13, 86, 91–93, 129, 135,
    137–139
    Galunggung (Indonesia) 88
    Kelut (Indonesia) 88
    lahar warning systems 137, 138
    Montserrat 93
    Mount Pinatubo (Philippines)
        136–137
    Mount Ruapehu (NZ) 138
    Mount St Helens (USA) 137
    Nevado del Ruiz (Colombia) 88,
        92, 139
    Nicaragua 138
    see also avalanches; landslides;
        mudflows
Lake Argentina 124

Lake Kivu (DRC) 89
Lake Monoun (Cameroon) 118, 119
Lake Nyos (Cameroon) 118–119
Lake Palca (Peru) 123
Lake Taupo (NZ) 84–85
lakes 18, 68, 84–85, 89, 115,
    118–119, 123, 124
    crater lakes 63, 68, 71, 84–85,
        87, 137, 138
    exploding lakes (Cameroon)
        118–119
    glacier lakes 122, 125
    lava lakes *see under* lava
landslides 4, 13, 51, 53, 58, 86,
    119, 129, 130–135, 144, 147,
    151
    California 132
    Huascarán (Peru) 130, 135, 144
    Réunion 130–131
    Santa Tecla (El Salvador) 5,
        132–133
    Yungay (Peru) 130
    see also avalanches; lahars;
        mudflows
Laurasia 34
lava 17, 18, 63, 66–69, 71, 80,
    82–83, 89–92, 95, 98, 99, 103,
    105, 106, 135
    andesitic lavas 75
    basaltic lavas 75, 77
    felsic lavas 74
    Hawaiian-style
        'a'a lava 75–77
        pahoehoe lava 75–77
    lava bombs 62, 71, 72, 78, 79,
        88, 107
    lava flows 5, 6, 74–77, 79, 83, 91,
        92, 95, 99, 105, 107
    lava fountains 69–71, 74, 75, 83
    lava lakes 71, 75, 76, 82, 83, 89
    lava rivers 70
    lava tubes 75, 76
    pillow lava 74, 76
Lebanon 24
Lesser Antilles 101
Lisbon 51, 55
lithosphere 20, 22–25, 27, 28, 38,
    96, 101
Lituya Bay (Alaska) 55
Lord Howe Seamount chain 99
Los Angeles 31, 44

M

maars 118
Macugnaga (Italy) 123
magma 16–18, 21–25, 27, 28,
    62–64, 66–68, 71, 73, 74, 76,
    78, 81, 82, 91, 93, 96, 101,
    105, 110, 118, 119
    magma chambers 27, 63, 68, 81,
        85, 91, 110
magnetism (Earth's) 32, 149
Malaysia 85, 127
Maldive Islands 99
mammals, placental 34, 35
Mammoth Hot Springs (USA) 112

Manila (Philippines) 58
mantle (Earth's) 17, 18, 20, 22–25, 27, 32, 34, 42, 63, 66, 85, 96, 101, 117, 151, 153
Mariana Islands 31, 101, 102–103
Marianas Trench 102
Marquesas Islands 99
marsupials 34, 35
Martinique 71, 87, 100, 101
Mauna Loa (Hawaii) 64, 71, 76, 96, 98
Mauritius 96, 99
Mayacamas Mountains (USA) 19
Mediterranean 39, 71, 91, 105, 106
Melanesia 31
Messina (Sicily) 51
methane gas 6, 109, 116, 120–121
Mexico 18, 31, 52, 64
Mexico City 31, 38, 48, 52, 53, 58, 59
Middle East 50, 51
Minami-iwo-jima (Japan) 106
Minoan culture, demise of 91
Modified Mercalli scale 43
Mojave Desert 135
Molokini (Hawaii) 99
moment magnitude scale 42, 43
Mönch, the (Switzerland) 145
Mont Pelée (Martinique) 71, 87, 88, 101
Montana 115
Monte Rosa (Italy) 123
Montserrat 3, 4, 80, 93, 100, 101
Moon 17, 127, 150
moraines 123, 125
Morocco 28
Mount Etna (Sicily) 5, 60–61, 65, 77, 90
Mount Katmai (Alaska) 81
Mount Nyiragongo (DRC) 65, 76, 89
Mount Pinatubo (Philippines) 30, 31, 72, 73, 93, 136–137
Mount Rainier (USA) 64, 137, 138, 145
Mount Ruapehu (NZ) 30, 137–138
Mount St Helens (USA) 12, 31, 71, 81, 86–88, 134, 137
Mount Unzen (Japan) 30, 65, 88
Mount Vesuvius (Italy) 18, 65, 70, 72, 73, 88, 90, 92–93
Mozambique 25, 82
mud, volcanic 109, 110, 112–114, 116–117
    mud volcanoes 13, 116–117, 120
    see also hot springs
mudflows 61, 79, 86, 88, 91, 129, 130, 134–139
    see also avalanches; lahars; landslides

N
Naples 92–93, 112
natrocarbonatite 83
natural gas 120
Nazca Plate 20, 23, 27, 31, 98, 99

Nepal 125
neutrons 148, 152, 153
Nevada 108–109, 115
Nevado del Ruiz (Colombia) 31, 88, 92, 139
Nevis 100
New Guinea 31
New Zealand 18, 30, 31, 84–85, 102, 110, 112–115, 137–138
Nicaragua 3, 4, 67, 138
nickel 17
Nicolosi (Sicily) 77
Ningxia-Gansu (China) 51
nitrogen 90, 116
Nojima Fault 32
North Africa 28
North America 34, 38, 51, 85
North American Plate 20–23, 26, 29, 31, 40, 52, 101
North Anatolian Fault 40
North Atlantic Plate 21
northern lights 154–155
nuclear power see under energy (Earth's)

O
Oakland (California) 44–45
oceans
    mid-ocean ridges 20, 21, 24, 25, 29, 32, 39, 64, 82, 99, 104, 105
    ocean floor 21, 29, 32, 34, 95, 105
        see also sea floor
    oceanic crust 20, 22–24, 27, 32
Okhotsk Plate 31
Ol Doinyo Lengai (Tanzania) 82–83
Old Faithful (Yellowstone) 114
Oregon 68
Osaka 49
outburst floods see under glaciers
oxygen 17, 112, 143, 154

P
P (primary) waves 42, 44
Pacific Ocean 22–23, 30–31, 39, 40, 55, 96, 98, 99, 101, 102, 106, 107
    East Pacific Rise 23, 24, 29
    'Ring of Fire' 30–31, 39, 40, 54, 103
Pacific Plate 20–23, 26, 29, 31, 32, 40, 102, 107
Pakistan 53, 142
Palouse Falls (USA) 123
Pamir Mountains (Tajikistan) 123
Pangaea 34
Papua New Guinea 30, 65
permafrost 131
Peru 31, 38, 123, 130, 144
Peru-Chile Trench 23
Philippines 18, 30, 31, 55, 58, 65, 72, 73, 93, 136–137
Philippines Plate 21, 31, 102
phosphorous 90

Pingvellir Fault (Iceland) 21
Piton des Neiges (Réunion) 99
plates, tectonic 14–15, 18, 20–35, 38, 147, 148, 151
    boundaries of 14, 15, 18, 20–29, 38, 40, 51–54, 98, 99, 101–103, 107, 110, 117
    constructive 22
    convergent 22, 27–28, 31, 54, 64, 68, 85, 101
    divergent 22–25, 29, 64, 82
    rift 21, 24–25, 64
    transform 22, 29
    and evolution 34–35
    movement of 13, 32
Pliny the Elder 73
Pliny the Younger 73, 88
plutonium 152
Plymouth (Montserrat) 93
Pompeii 70, 88
potassium 18, 90, 153
power plants 19, 115
protons 148, 152–154
Puget Sound (USA) 137
Pulau Seduku (Sarawak) 127
pumice 88, 103, 135
Punakha (Bhutan) 123
pyroclastic flows 3, 63, 71, 72, 80–81, 86–88, 91, 93, 137, 139
    Galunggung (Indonesia) 138
    Mont Pelée (Martinique) 88
    Mount Vesuvius (Italy) 88

QR
Qiantang Jiang bore 127
radioactivity 17–18, 148, 152, 153
    radioactive decay 13, 18, 149, 152, 153
radon gas 57
rain 3, 110, 119, 132, 134, 137–140, 151
Ranrahirca (Peru) 144
Red Sea 25
Reghaia (Algeria) 53
rescue workers 39, 48, 53, 141, 143
respiratory problems 79
Réunion 96, 99, 130–131
Richter scale 4, 42, 43, 73
ridges, mid-ocean see under oceans
rift valleys 21, 24, 25, 82, 83
rift zones 25, 64, 67
'Ring of Fire' (Pacific Ocean) 30–31, 39, 40, 54, 103
rivers 127
rock falls 13, 129, 130, 134, 138
Rodrigues Island 99
Rolando Rodriguez (Nicaragua) 138
Romania 117
Rota (Mariana Islands) 102
Rotorua (NZ) 112
Russia 26, 31, 65, 72
Ryukyu Islands (Japan) 103

S
S (secondary) waves 42, 44, 47
Saas Fee (Switzerland) 144
St Kitts 100
St Lucia 100
Saint-Pierre 71, 87
St Vincent 100
Saipan (Mariana Islands) 102, 103
San Andreas Fault 20, 29, 51
San Bernadino Range 135
San Francisco 29, 36–38, 47, 48, 51, 58
San Salvador (El Salvador) 58
Santa Tecla (El Salvador) 5, 132–133
Sarawak 127
Satellite Laser Ranging (SLR) 32
Scarborough 134
scoria 104, 105
Scotia Plate 20
scree 134
sea floor 6, 24, 32, 54, 96, 101, 102, 104, 105, 107, 121, 135
    see also under oceans
seamounts 96, 99
Seattle 137
seismic activity 38, 42, 58, 91
seismology 42, 56, 59, 91, 137
Severn bore 126–127
Shaanxi (China) 51
Shasta Valley (California) 135
Sicily 5, 51, 65, 71, 77, 90, 105
silica (silicon dioxide) 68, 114
silicon 17
skiing 143
skyscrapers 58
snow 4, 92, 110, 123, 128–129, 134, 135, 137, 140–143
Society Islands 99
soil
    soil liquefaction 46–47, 52, 58
    soil movement 131–134
solar radiation 142
Solar System 16, 17
solifluction (soil movement) 131
Solomon Islands 4, 6, 30, 31, 39, 103, 107
South America 23, 27, 32, 34, 35, 101
South American Plate 20–21, 23, 27, 31, 101
South Pole 34
Southern Ocean 24
Spitak (Armenia) 39
springs see hot springs
Sri Aman (Sarawak) 127
Sri Lanka 6
steam, volcanic 81, 91, 93, 105, 107, 112–114
Stromboli 71
subduction zones 20, 22, 23, 27, 28, 30, 31, 51, 101
subsidence 52
Sudan 82
Sulawesi 88
sulphur 103, 107, 112, 114

sulphur dioxide 79, 91, 112
sulphuric acid 102, 112, 113
Sumatra 4, 6, 18, 30, 51, 85, 88, 103
Sumbawa (Indonesia) 88
Sun 16, 151, 154
Sunda Strait 88
Sunda volcanic arc 27, 103
Surtsey (Iceland) 91, 104–105
Svalbard 144
Switzerland 144, 145
Syria 24, 25, 51

T
Tacoma (USA) 137
Taipei 46-7
Tajikistan 123
talus 134
Tangshan (China) 39, 51, 52, 56
Tanzania 82–83
Tashkent (Uzbekistan) 58
Taupo volcanic zone (NZ) 84–85, 114
tectonic plates see plates, tectonic
Tenerife 65
Thailand 6
The Geysers (California) 19
thorium 18, 153
Tibetan Plateau 28
tidal bores 126–127
tidal energy see under energy (Earth's)
Tinian (Mariana Islands) 102
Tofua volcanic arc 103
Tokyo 51, 56–58
Tonga 102, 103, 106
Torre Mayor building 59
trenches, oceanic 23, 27, 101, 102
Trinidad 117
Tristan da Cunha 99
Troy 50
Tsho Rolpa Glacier Lake (Nepal) 125
Tsinghai (China) 51
tsunamis 37, 50, 54, 61, 88, 92, 101, 135, 137
  Indian Ocean (2004) 6, 12, 27, 51, 54–55
  Japan 55, 88
  Krakatau (Indonesia) 88
  Lisbon 55
  Lituya Bay (Alaska) 55
  Mediterranean 91
  megatsunamis 55
  Mount Unzen (Japan) 88
Turkey 40–41
Turkmenistan 51

UV
Unzen (Japan) 65, 88
uranium 18, 152, 153
USA 12, 18, 64, 68, 71, 85, 86–87, 110, 112, 114, 123, 134, 135, 137, 145
Uzbekistan 58

Valley of Ten Thousand Smokes, The 81
Vanuatu 103
Vatnajökull (Iceland) 3, 122
Venezuela 117
volcanic eruptions 12, 15, 16, 60–123, 147, 151, 152
  deadliest 88
  exploding lakes 118–119
  island eruptions 94–107
  killer eruptions 86–89
  predictions of 90, 91, 93
  styles of 70–73
    Hawaiian 70–71
    Icelandic 70–71
    Pelean 71, 72
    Phreatic 71–72
    Plinian 72, 73, 91
      ultra-Plinian 73
    Strombolian 71
    Vesuvian 72–73
    Vulcanian 72
  subglacial 122, 123
  see also geysers; hot springs; mud, volcanic; volcanic islands; volcanoes
Volcanic Explosivity Index (VEI) 73, 81, 84, 86, 88, 91
volcanic islands 18, 22, 23, 27, 30–32, 71, 74, 79, 80, 87, 91, 93, 94–107
  Atlantic 96, 99, 100–101, 135
  Caribbean 71, 80, 87, 93, 100–102
  hotspot islands 23, 32, 96–99, 104, 105
  Indian Ocean 99
  Indonesian 27, 71, 85, 88, 103
  Japanese 27, 30, 31, 65, 101, 103, 106
  Mediterranean 71, 72, 105, 106
  Pacific 22, 23, 27, 30–31, 96, 99, 101, 102–103, 106, 107
  in 'Ring of Fire' 30–31
  see also Galápagos Islands; Hawaii; Iceland; Mariana Islands; Solomon Islands; volcanic eruptions; volcanoes
Volcano Island (Japan) 103
volcanoes 16, 18, 22–31, 60–107, 109, 123, 132, 134, 135, 137–138
  active volcanoes 64
  Agrihan (Mariana Islands) 102
  airborne hazards from 78–79
  Alcedo (Galápagos) 97
  Aleutian Islands 30
  Antahan (Mariana Islands) 102
  Arenal (Costa Rica) 68
  ash see ash, volcanic
  Avachinsky (Russia) 65
  Baku (Azerbaijan) 117
  Bandai (Japan) 72
  caldera volcanoes 66, 68
  Casita (Nicaragua) 3, 138
  Cerro Negro (Nicaragua) 67

cinder cone volcanoes 66, 67, 71
cinders see cinders, volcanic
Colima (Mexico) 31, 64
composite volcanoes 66, 68, 71–73, 75, 83, 88, 89, 137, 138
Costa Rica 31, 68
Cumbre Vieja (La Palma) 135
Darwin (Galápagos) 97
deadliest eruptions 88
dormant volcanoes 64
Empedocles 106
Erta Ale (Ethiopia) 17, 67, 82, 83
extinct volcanoes 64
Fiji 30
Fukutoku-Okanoba (Japan) 103, 106
Galeras (Colombia) 31, 64, 79
Galunggung (Indonesia) 88, 138
Hatepe (NZ) 85
Iriomote-jima (Ryukyu Islands) 103
Kamchatka (Russia) 26, 30
Karymsky (Russia) 72
Kavachi (Solomon Islands) 6, 107
Kelut (Indonesia) 88, 138
Kermadec Islands 30
Kick'em Jenny (Caribbean) 101–102
Kilauea (Hawaii) 69, 71, 75, 96, 98
killer eruptions 86–89
Kliuchevskoi (Kamchatka) 30
Krakatau (Indonesia) 71, 88
La Cumbre (Galápagos) 96–97
La Garita (USA) 85
La Grande Soufrière (Guadeloupe) 101
Laki (Iceland) 88
lava see lava
living with 90–93
Loihi (Hawaii) 98
magma see magma
Mauna Kea (Hawaii) 96
Mauna Loa (Hawaii) 64, 71, 76, 96, 98
Merapi (Indonesia) 65
Minami-Hiyoshi (Japan) 103
mini-volcanoes 63
Mont Pelée (Martinique) 71, 87, 88, 101
Mount Erebus (Antarctica) 78–79
Mount Etna (Sicily) 5, 60–61, 65, 77, 90
Mount Katmai (Alaska) 81
Mount Manam (Papua New Guinea) 30
Mount Nyiragongo (DRC) 65, 76, 89
Mount Pinatubo (Philippines) 30, 31, 72, 73, 93, 136–137
Mount Rainier (USA) 64, 137, 138
Mount Ruapehu (NZ) 30, 137–138

Mount St Helens (USA) 12, 31, 71, 81, 86–88, 134, 137
Mount Shasta (USA) 64, 135
Mount Spurr (Alaska) 30
Mount Tambora (Indonesia) 88
Mount Unzen (Japan) 30, 65, 88
Mount Vesuvius (Italy) 18, 65, 70, 72, 73, 88, 90, 92–93
mud volcanoes see under mud, volcanic
Nevado del Ruiz (Colombia) 31, 88, 92, 139
Nyamuragira (DRC) 70
Ol Doinyo Lengai (Tanzania) 82–83
Oruanui (NZ) 84–85
Pagan (Mariana Islands) 102
Pico del Teide (Tenerife) 65
Piton des Neiges (Réunion) 99
pyroclastic flows see pyroclastic flows
rift volcanoes 82–83
in 'Ring of Fire' 30–31
Rota-1 (Mariana Islands) 102, 103
Ruby (Mariana Islands) 103
Sabancaya (Peru) 31
Sakurajima (Japan) 65
Santa Maria (Guatemala) 64
Santorini (Greece) 65, 91
shield volcanoes 66–67, 69, 71, 75, 76
Solomon Islands 30
Soufrière Hills (Montserrat) 3, 80, 93, 101
submarine volcanoes 6, 13, 76, 95, 96, 98, 101–107
super-volcanoes 18, 84–85
Surtsey (Iceland) 104–105
Taal (Philippines) 65
Toba, Lake (Sumatra) 18, 85
Tungurahua (Ecuador) 62
types of 66–68
Ulawun (Papua New Guinea) 65
Villarrica (Chile) 31
Wolf (Galápagos) 97
see also volcanic eruptions; volcanic islands
volcanologists 90, 91, 93
Vulcano (Sicily) 72

WY
Washington State 71, 86–87, 123, 134, 137, 145
waves 54, 55, 107, 127, 134
West Africa 118–119
West Virginia 121
Whakarewarewa Thermal Reserve (NZ) 110–112
White Island (NZ) 102
wind energy see under energy (Earth's)
Wyoming 85, 112, 114
Yellowstone N.P. 85, 112, 114, 115
Yokohama (Japan) 51
Yungay (Peru) 130

PICTURE CREDITS

Abbreviations: T = top; B = bottom; L = left; R = right

Front Cover: Olivier Grunwald.
Back Cover: Corbis/Tom Bean.

1 Olivier Grunewald. **2 & 7** Robert Harding/Robert Francis. **3** Still Pictures/Juan Pablo Moreiras/FFI, T; Still Pictures © Ullstein–LS–PRESS, M; National Geographic Image Collection/SteveWinter, B. **4** Rex Features/Sipa Press, L; Getty Images/AFP, R. **5** PA Photos/AP, L; National Geographic Collection/Carsten Peters, R. **6** Camera Press/Gamma/XINHUA, T; PA Photos/Gemunu Amarasinghe/AP, M; Getty Images/AFP, B. **8–9** Olivier Grunewald. **10** Corbis/Yann Arthus–Bertrand, TL; PA Photos/AP, TR; Science Photo Library/Bernhard Edmaier, BL; Camera Press/Gamma/Aventurier-Loviny, BR. **11** Corbis, TL; Arcticphoto.com/Ragnar Th Sigurosson, TR; Arcticphoto.com/Bryan & Cherry Alexander, B. **12** Photolibrary.com/Picture Press/Gerhard Schulz, TL; National Geographic Image Collection/Carsten Peter, TM. **12–13** Science Photo Library/Bernhard Edmaier, M; Auscape International/Tui de Roi, background. **13** Oceans-image.com/Charles Hood, TM; Hedgehog House/Ingrid Visser, TR. **14–15** Oceans-image.com/Charles Hood. **16** Olivier Grunewald. **17** Shutterstock/Nikolajs Strigins. **19** Science Photo Library/Jack Fields. **20** Corbis/Yann Arthus-Bertrand. **21** Corbis/Yann Arthus-Bertrand, T; naturepl.com/Anup Shah, B. **23** European Space Agency, T. **24** NASA/Shuttle Mission. **25** Science Photo Library/Dr Ken MacDonald, B. **26–27** National Geographic Image Collection/Carsten Peter. **28** NASA/JPL, B. **29** Corbis/Tom Bean, R. **30** Corbis/Noburu Hashimoto, TL; Auscape International/Tui De Roy, BL. **31** Getty Images/Schafer & Hill. **33** Rex Features/Roy Garner. **35** Auscape International/Jean-Paul Ferrero, T; © National Library of Wales, B. **36–37** PA Photos/AP. **38** FLPA/Steve McCutcheon, BR. **39** Panos/Chris Stowers, T; Corbis/Peter Turnley, B. **40–41** Reuters/Marine Expeditionary Unit. **44** Reuters/Blake Sell. **44–45** PA Photos/Paul Sakuma. **46–47** Reuters/Simon Kwong. **46** Corbis Sygma/Noburu Hashimoto, TR. **48** AFP. **49** Reuters/Kimimasa Mayama. **50–51** Corbis/Reuters/Jason Reed. **52** PA Photos/AP/Amir Qureshi, L; PA Photos/AP/Hasan Sarbakhshian, R. **53** PA Photos/AP/Nabil, C; Getty Images/AFP/Omar Torres, R. **54–55** Reuters. **56** Steinbrugge Collection, EERC, University of California, Berkeley/T. Kuribayashi. **56–57** Aurora Photos/Peter Essick. **57** Getty Images/AFP/Toru Yamanaka, TR. **58** Aurora Photos/Peter Essick, B. **58–59** Alamy Images/Dyana. **59** Aurora Photos/Peter Essick, TR. **60–61** National Geographic Image Collection/Carsten Peter. **62–63** Corbis/Pablo Corral Vega. **64** Corbis/epa, B. **65** Photolibrary.com/JTB Photo, T; Shutterstock/Natalia Sinjushina, B. **66–67** Science Photo Library/Ray Fairbanks. **67** National Geographic Image Collection/Carsten Peter, B. **68** Photolibrary.com/Brian P. Kenney, T; National Geographic Image Collection/Raymond Gehman, BL. **69** Corbis. **70** National Geographic Image Collection/Chris Johns. **71** Science Photo Library/Explorer/Krafft. **72** National Geographic Image Collection/Klaus Nigge, L; Still Pictures/UNEP/Robert T. Wells, R. **73** Corbis/Bettmann. **74** SeaPics.com/Doug Perrine. **75** Science Photo Library/Dan Suzio, TL; Corbis/Roger

Ressmeyer, BR. **76** Corbis/J. D. Griggs. **77** Robert Harding/Robert Francis. **78–79** Science Photo Library/George Steinmetz. **79** National Geographic Image Collection/Robert S. Patton. **80** Panos/Andy Johnstone. **81** Robert Harding/A.C. Waltham. **82–83** National Geographic Image Collection/Carsten Peter. **83** Olivier Grunewald. **84–85** Auscape International/Jean-Marc La Roque. **85** Science Photo Library/CNES, 2001 Distribution Spot Image. **86–87** US Geological Survey, T; Science Photo Library/US Geological Survey, B. **89** Auscape International/Maurice & Katia Krafft. **90** PA Photos/AP/Pier Paolo Cito. **91** Corbis/Bob Krist. **92–93** Corbis/Roger Ressmeyer. **94–95** Auscape International/Tui De Roy. **97** Science Photo Library/CNES, 1988 Distribution Spot Image. **98** NOAA Photo Library/G. McMurtry/OAR/National Undersea Research Program, University of Hawaii. **99** National Geographic Image Collection/Chris Johns. **100** NASA/GSFC/Jacques Descloitres, MODIS Rapid Response Team. **102–103** Hedgehog House/Ingrid Visser. **103** PA Photos/PA Archive. **104** Corbis Sygma/Pierre Vauthey, L; Corbis, R. **105** Arcticphoto.com/Ragnar Th Sigurosson. **106** Corbis/Reuters/Handout/Japan Coast Guard. **107** Getty Images/AFP. **108–109** Photolibrary.com/Picture Press/Gerhard Schulz. **111** Science Photo Library/Bernhard Edmaier. **112** DRK Photo/Steve Kaufman. **112–113** Science Photo Library/Bernhard Edmaier. **114** Science Photo Library/Simon Fraser. **115** Olivier Grunewald L; DRK Photo/Thomas Dressler R. **116–117** Corbis/Wolfgang Kaehler. **118–119** Corbis/Thierry Orban. **119** AFP/Desirey Minkoh. **120–121** Corbis/epa/Chongwan. **121** Reuters/China Photos. **122–123** Photolibrary.com/Nordicphotos/Kristjan Maack. **123** David Jensen. **124** Science Photo Library/NASA, T; Corbis/Reuters/Carlos Corvalan/Intendecia El Calafate B. **125** Corbis/Reuters/Carlos Corvalan/Intendecia El Calafate. **126–127** © mhWeather/Mark Humpage. **128–129** Corbis/Reuters/ARC. **130–131** Camera Press/Gamma/Imaz Press. **132** PA Photos/AP/Nick Ut. **132–133** Reuters. **134** PA Photos/PA Archive/John Giles. **135** Corbis © Roger Ressmeyer. **136–137** Camera Press/Gamma/Aventurier-Loviny. **138** Reuters/Anthony Phelps. **139** Corbis Sygma/Jacques Langevin. **140–141** Austrian Armed Forces Photograph. **142** Hedgehog House/Kynan Bazley. **143** Alamy/Extreme Sports Photo. **144–145** Getty Images/Michael Melford. **146–147** PA Photos/AP/Filip Horvat. **148** Corbis/Doug Wilson, L: Science Photo Library/US Department of Energy, R. **149** Arcticphoto.com/Bryan & Cherry Alexander. **150–151** Corbis/Doug Wilson. **152** Science Photo Library/US Department of Energy. **154** PA Photos/Hertfordshire Police. **155** Arcticphoto.com/Bryan & Cherry Alexander.

Artworks:
Bradbury and Williams: 34, 148, 149TR, 153
Bradbury and Williams/Mountain High: 30–31, 38–39, 64–65
Glyn Walton: 17, 20–21, 22–23, 24–25, 27, 28, 29, 30–31, 38BL, 40, 42, 43, 59, 63, 67, 68, 101, 110

NATURE'S MIGHTY POWERS: EARTH'S EXPLOSIVE ENERGY was published by The Reader's Digest Association Ltd, London. It was created and produced for Reader's Digest by Toucan Books Ltd, London.

The Reader's Digest Association Ltd,
11 Westferry Circus,
Canary Wharf,
London E14 4HE
www.readersdigest.co.uk

First edition copyright © 2008

Written by
Robert Dinwiddie

FOR TOUCAN BOOKS

Editors Jane Chapman, Celia Coyne, Helen Douglas-Cooper, Andrew Kerr-Jarrett
Designers Bradbury & Williams
Picture researchers Wendy Brown, Sharon Southren, Mia Stewart-Wilson, Christine Vincent, Caroline Wood
Proofreader Marion Dent
Indexer Michael Dent

FOR READER'S DIGEST
Project editor Christine Noble
Art editor Julie Bennett
Pre-press account manager Penny Grose, Dean Russell
Product production manager Claudette Bramble
Production controller Katherine Bunn

READER'S DIGEST, GENERAL BOOKS
Editorial director Julian Browne
Art director Anne-Marie Bulat

Colour origination Colour Systems Ltd, London
Printed and bound in China

We are committed to both the quality of our products and the service we provide to our customers. We value your comments, so please feel free to contact us on 08705 113366 or via our website at **www.readersdigest.co.uk**

If you have any comments or suggestions about the content of our books, you can email us at **gbeditorial@readersdigest.co.uk**

CONCEPT CODE: UK0138/G/S
BOOK CODE: 636-007 UP0000-1
ISBN: 978-0-276-44295-7
ORACLE CODE: 356500014H.00.24